# ELECTRIC
# BREAD®

## A BREAD MACHINE ACTIVITY BOOK

### for

Another product from Innovative Cooking Enterprises, I.C.E., Inc.
Anchorage, Alaska

Published and Developed by:

# Innovative Cooking Enterprises * I.C.E., Inc.

Cover, Book Design & Photography by:
## Art & International Productions, LLC
### Anchorage, Alaska

Book Production Team:
(LEFT TO RIGHT)
Ann McKay Bryson, Jim Tilly, John McKay,
Mary Ann Swalling, Oleg Parshin, Ann Parrish

Copyright © 1998 by Innovative Cooking Enterprises * I.C.E., Inc.

***ELECTRIC BREAD*** is a registered trademark of
Innovative Cooking Enterprises * I.C.E., Inc.

**Published by**
Innovative Cooking Enterprises * I.C.E., Inc.
P. O. Box 240888 Anchorage, Alaska 99524-0888

SAN 297-441X
*First Printing, August, 1998*
Printed in China
Library of Congress Catalog Card Number: 98-72726
ISBN 1-891705-00-8

# TABLE OF CONTENTS

# FUN THINGS TO MAKE!

# BREAD BAKER'S BASICS

# HOW IT ALL BEGAN...

**W**e thought you might like to know just a little about how we at Innovative Cooking Enterprises (ICE) came to create this book for you…

In June 1996 when Martin McKay was turning nine years old, he discovered an enormous gift box in the family room. He tore it open, only to find another, slightly smaller wrapped package inside. Martin opened box after nesting box until all that was left was … an envelope, containing a note announcing, "A PARTY! Bring your friends to the Electric Bread Test Kitchen!"

Martin was jazzed. His mom, Suzan Nightingale, had been the writer on the team that created the best-selling bread machine cookbook, *Electric Bread*®. He and his younger brother, Cameron, had tried the delicious bread recipes the grown-ups developed at the test kitchen of Innovative Cooking Enterprises. They had also visited the test kitchen several times, but they had never been "turned loose" in it.

When she wrapped that box, ICE President Ann Parrish knew Martin and his buddies would have a great party. They'd have fun making individual pizzas, creating their own bread alligators, and baking loaves of chocolate bread. Ann was a recognized leader in the bread machine industry and ran a company from Anchorage, Alaska, that reached into kitchens around the world. But this didn't prepare her for how much fun it would be when kids hit the test kitchen, or how it would change our company.

We've baked over **30,000 loaves** at ICE's test kitchen in Anchorage, Alaska. We've created and tested the gourmet recipes here for our books *Electric Bread* and *More Electric Bread*, that have sold nearly a million copies. We knew how adults enjoyed using our recipes in the bread machine to make successful bread. But, how would kids take to it?

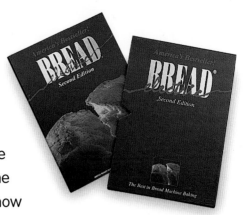

Like chocolate to a chip. Like a bun takes to a burger. Kids left Martin's party saying it was the best ever. All the boys and girls had so much fun, and were so successful, that it was obvious our test kitchen would never be the same. Bread machine baking was clearly something for the whole family to enjoy. So, the idea for *Electric Bread for Kids* was born, and the rest is history — and fun, and science, and fun, and baking, and fun, and art, and fun....

Before we could turn the idea into this book, we had to squeeze in a lot more fun. We invited thirty kids to come into our test kitchen in focus groups to try recipes and baking techniques, and to invent their own creations. A few knew their way around a kitchen, but most had never used a bread machine or made things from dough

before. They ranged in age from kindergarten to middle school. Every one did great work, and had a great time. Each item you see in this book was baked and shaped by these kids.

### And if they can do it, you can too!

# SECRETS TO SUCCESS

This chapter shares the most important secrets you need to become a great baker.

Most breads have their own special hints or tips. You will find these hints on each recipe or activity page.

Some secrets apply to <u>everything</u> you do with your bread machine. Like a foundation for a building, they are the first and most important part. Once you know these secrets, using your bread machine will be easy and your creations will be a joy to make, bake and share.

Before you jump into the fun, read all the pages in this chapter. You'll find the most important stuff about:

- Safety,
- Tools and Equipment,
- Getting to Know Your Machine,
- Using This Book,
- Measuring, and
- Basic Dough Techniques.

Then you'll be ready to discover and enjoy many wonderful baking experiences....

**Feedback...** We'd love to hear from you. Tell us what you like about *Electric Bread for Kids* and your baking adventures. Send us pictures of some of the bread art you create. You can e-mail us at kids@electricbread.com or mail to Innovative Cooking Enterprises, P.O. Box 240888, Anchorage, Alaska, 99524-0888.

# SAFETY

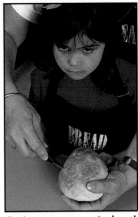

## Kids:

We use this symbol as a reminder that you should be alert, and that an adult helper is needed. When you use our book, HAVE FUN. Enjoy yourself. But while all you worry about is how good the bread will taste, here are the kinds of things grown-ups worry about: When you are taking bread out of the oven, or out of the loaf pan of your bread machine, you could burn yourself. When you use a knife, you could slice or dice yourself. When you handle the plug of your machine with wet hands near an electrical outlet, or if the cat or an earthquake knocks your bread machine into a sinkful of water, you could shock yourself. In fact, if you use a breadstick incorrectly, you could poke your eye out. PLEASE DON'T. Please don't burn, cut, shock, or otherwise hurt yourself. But if you do, don't say we didn't warn you. We just did. If you are working around things that are sharp or hot or dangerous be alert and ask an adult for help. **Besides, adults like it when you talk to them, and it will be a good way to get them back into the kitchen.**

Quinsey, age 6, had hoped to cut the top off the soup bowl herself, but Mary Ann, her adult helper kept Quinsey's fingers safe.

# Be Careful....

Using your bread machine is safer than watching TV, plus it smells better and is better for you. But here are a few basic safety tips to keep in mind.

#  KEEP IT CLEAN

We keep our mold and bacteria in the science section of our Electric Bread Goes to School chapter. Clean hands, utensils, and kitchen surfaces will help keep them out of your bread and dough:

- Wash your hands before you start baking, after every time you sneeze, every time you handle eggs, and every time you pet your dog or cat. We're not talking about passing your hands under a dripping faucet within sight of a bar of soap. Wash your hands thoroughly, scrubbing them with soap, for at least 30 seconds (enough time to sing the alphabet song) and then rinse well.
- Keep your clothes clean and feel like a professional by wearing an apron.
- Replace lids tightly, and be sure to put away cold foods such as milk, butter, and yeast, promptly.
- Keep paper towels handy. Wipe up spills right away.
- Don't use the same cloth for the floor as for countertops and dishes.
- Leave your kitchen cleaner than you found it.

#  FOLLOW BREAD MACHINE SAFETY TIPS

While you come to think of your bread machine as your best friend, remember that it is still an electrical appliance:

- As with any electrical appliance, never plug in or unplug your bread machine with wet hands.
- Don't put your hand or a utensil in the bread machine while it's mixing.
- Your bread machine is an oven. The bread pan is very hot when the bread finishes baking. Let an adult lift the pan out of the machine and shake the bread out of the pan.
- If the kneading blade sticks inside your loaf, remember it is hot. Have an adult take it out.
- To unplug the bread machine, take hold of the plug, not the cord, and pull it straight out.

The heating element of your bread machine is "red hot" during baking.

#  SLICE, CHOP AND GRATE WITH CAUTION

No adventure in the kitchen can be considered a complete success unless you finish with as many fingers and as much blood as you started with, so:

- Have an adult slice your bread.
- Be careful with knives. Always use the handle; never touch the blade.
- Always chop or slice food on a cutting board, not when holding the food in your hand.
- Wash knives separately.
- When grating cheese watch your fingertips and knuckles, and don't get your hand too close to the grater surface.
- When the piece of cheese gets small, replace it with a larger one.

#  OBEY OVEN ETIQUETTE

Indian mystics have trained their minds and bodies so they can walk across burning coals. We're wimps in the burning coals department, so we avoid letting skin come into contact with burning hot things or fire:

- An adult should be present anytime you are using an oven, or should teach you how to use the oven when they think you're ready to do this on your own.
- If you need to adjust the oven rack, do it when the oven is cold.
- Always use thick, dry potholders or oven mitts.
- If there is ever a fire, yell for your grown-up immediately.
- Always turn off the oven as soon as you're done using it. (It's easy to forget.)
- And, while your table and cupboards don't scream if they get burned, you should still care. Set hot pans on a trivet, hot pad, or cooling rack in a safe place where no one will bump them.

# TOOLS AND EQUIPMENT

With these tools and equipment you can make the breads in our book. Check the tool list shown at the top of the page for each dough recipe or activity before you begin. Remember to take care of your tools by using them safely and keeping them clean.

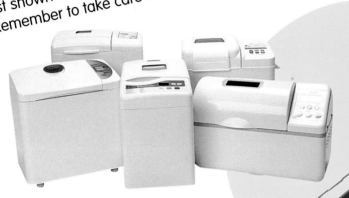

**Bread Machines**

**Bread Machine Kneading Blades**

**Machine Bread Pans**

**Liquid Measuring Cups**

**Measuring Spoons**

**Dry Measuring Cups**

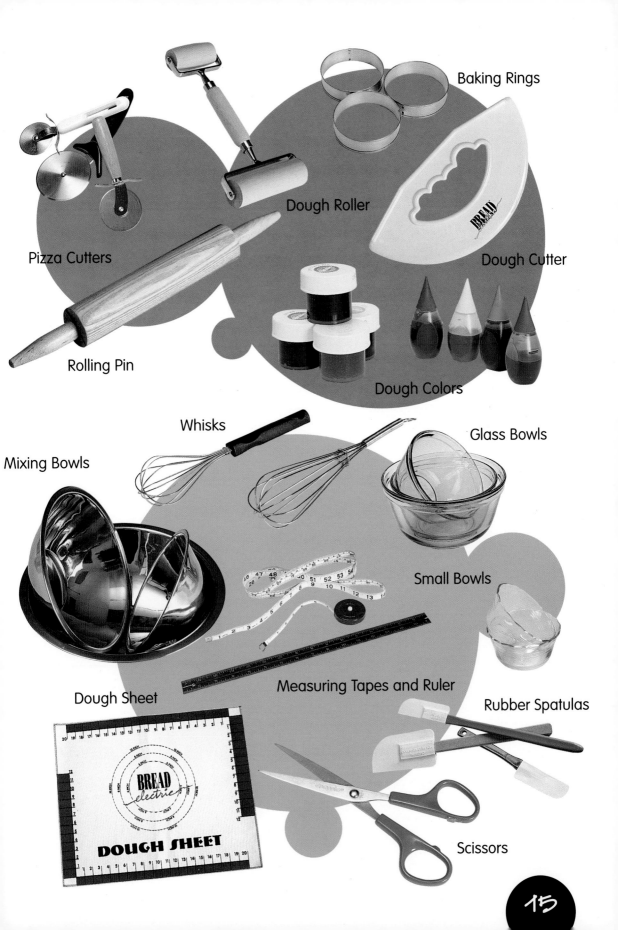

Pizza Cutters

Dough Roller

Baking Rings

Dough Cutter

Rolling Pin

Dough Colors

Whisks

Glass Bowls

Mixing Bowls

Small Bowls

Measuring Tapes and Ruler

Dough Sheet

Rubber Spatulas

BREAD
electric
DOUGH SHEET

Scissors

15

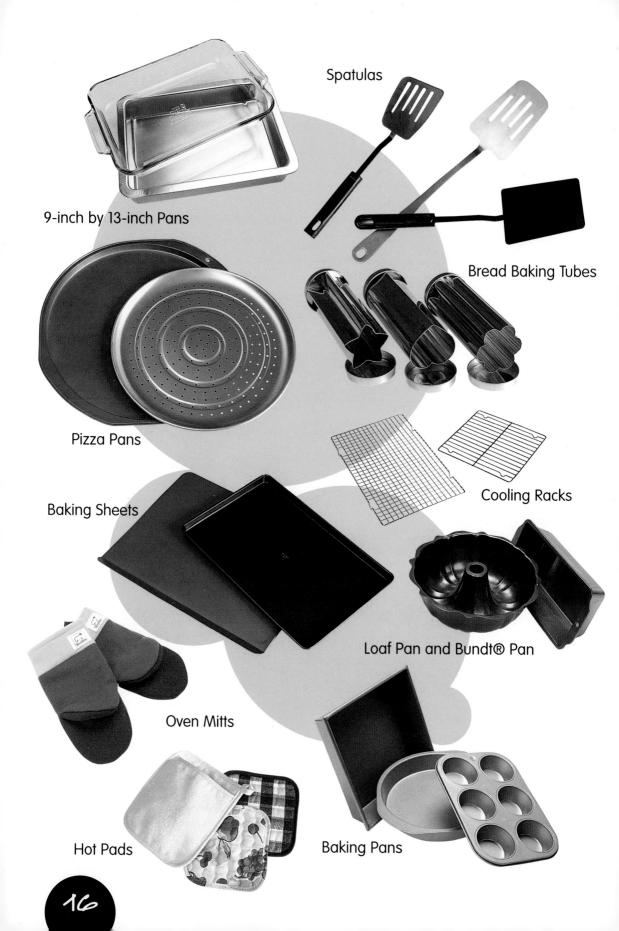

Spatulas

9-inch by 13-inch Pans

Bread Baking Tubes

Pizza Pans

Cooling Racks

Baking Sheets

Loaf Pan and Bundt® Pan

Oven Mitts

Hot Pads

Baking Pans

16

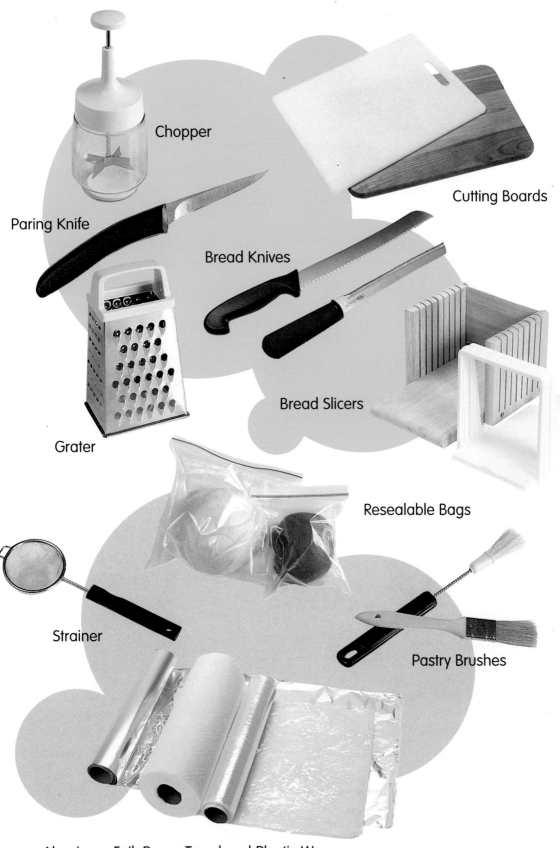

Chopper

Cutting Boards

Paring Knife

Bread Knives

Grater

Bread Slicers

Resealable Bags

Strainer

Pastry Brushes

Aluminum Foil, Paper Towel and Plastic Wrap

# YOUR BREAD MACHINE...

All bread machines can make good bread, but they are not all alike. We have over 200 bread machine models in our test kitchen and our kids learned how to use many different kinds. Fortunately, you only need to become familiar with the bread machine you'll be using. Before you start baking, have your adult helper show you how your machine works. Be sure to find out about:

## YOUR CONTROL UNIT...

The buttons to start the machine and select the cycles are located here. Find the start and stop buttons. Learn the cycle names and approximate baking times. (The recipes in our book work on cycles common to most machines: white, whole

wheat, French and sweet.) With the empty pan in the machine, practice choosing the cycle, starting the machine and then stopping it.

## YOUR "DELAY BAKE"...

It's fun to enjoy fresh warm bread in the morning or when you get home from school. Some machines allow you to pre-set the machine to bake up to 16 hours later. If your machine has a "delay bake" cycle, practice setting it to have the bread come out several hours later than the basic white bread cycle.

## YOUR DOUGH CYCLE...

All our Simply Delicious Recipes can be either baked as a loaf in the machine or removed and hand shaped for dough projects. For everything else in the book, you will only use the machine to make dough. If your machine has a special dough cycle, you'll remove the dough at the end of this cycle. If your machine doesn't have a dough cycle, check your machine's manual and write down how long it takes to complete the first knead. Start your machine using the regular cycle and when this amount of time is up, push the stop button and remove the dough.

## YOUR BREAD PAN...

Some pans are trickier than others. Some need to be "locked in" and some require a sturdy push to get them in all the way.

When your machine is cool, practice removing the empty bread pan and then placing it back in the machine. That way when the pan is full of ingredients, your job will be easy and you won't spill!

## YOUR FIRST LOAF...

Select a basic recipe like White Bread (Page 30) or French (Page 38 ). Read the entire recipe before you begin. Place all the ingredients you need on the counter in the same order as shown in the recipe. As you finish adding each ingredient, put it away. That way, you'll detect anything you left out and get a head start on clean-up. Measure carefully and remember to add liquid ingredients first and the yeast last, away from all moisture. Dried fruits should also be placed away from liquids.

## OPENING YOUR MACHINE...

Check your bread machine five to ten minutes after the mixing starts to make sure all your ingredients have been pulled down into the dough and it's mixing properly. If there is a problem, stop the machine, remove the pan to the counter and push the ingredients down with a rubber spatula. Replace the pan and then start the machine again.

Once the baking has started do not open your machine. Remember, the bread machine is an oven. Opening the door will let cooler air in and keep your loaf from baking evenly. No peeking while baking!

# ABOUT THIS BOOK...

## RECIPE SIZE...

The recipes in our book are family-sized and work in bread machines that make one and one-half pound or larger loaves. Bread machines produce different loaf sizes because of the differences in bread pan shapes, bread pan capacities (how much it holds) and the recipes used.

To make our recipes work in machines with different shapes and sizes of pans, each Simply Delicious Recipe page gives two recipes…titled "A" and "B".

To find out if "A" or "B" is right for you, first determine the shape of your bread pan (cylinder, square or rectangle). Then use a liquid measuring cup to measure water into your bread pan, keeping track of the total cups needed to fill the machine's bread pan to the brim. ⚠ Have your adult helper empty the bread pan.

Now use the chart below. Find the cups of water your bread pan holds on the chart. On that row, go to the column for your machine's pan shape. At the point where your pan's capacity and shape meet, the letter "A" or "B" is shown. This is the Simply Delicious Recipe for your machine. "A" is shown on the left side of the recipe page and the "B" recipe is on the right side. Make sure to use the recipe labeled with the letter shown for your machine every time you bake.

| Pan Capacity (In Cups of Water) | Pan Shape | | |
|---|---|---|---|
| | Cylinder | Square | Rectangle |
| 10 to 12 Cups | A | A | A |
| 12 to 16 Cups | A | A | B |
| More than 16 Cups | B | B | B |

# YEAST MEASUREMENTS...

Our recipes give two different yeast measurements — so you can use the yeast of your choice. There are two types of granulated yeast used in bread machines. Each works differently in the recipe. The traditional yeast is called "active dry," while bread machine or rapid rise yeast is known as "fast rise."

In our recipes, the "fast rise" measurement is shown first and the "active dry" measurement last. Find out which yeast you have and then use the correct measurement. Only use one type of yeast in each recipe.

**Yeast**
fast rise
2 teaspoons
-or-
**Yeast**
active dry
3 teaspoons

# NUTRITIONAL INFORMATION...

For the health conscious young baker, nutritional information is included for our Simply Delicious Recipes. This nutritional information is based on 12 servings of the "A" recipe. The size of finished breads from our dough recipes and activities were varied. Nutritional content of these breads will depend on the individual young baker's cutting, spreading, and decorating talents.

# "BAKER'S CHOICE"...

**DOUGH**

**Baker's Choice**

- **White Bread**
- **Garlic Bread**
- **Multigrain Bread**
- **Other...**

One thing we learned in the test kitchen was that each kid has their own idea of which dough should be used or which topping should go in or onto their own creation. To give you "creative freedom," some recipes contain a BAKER'S CHOICE section with a list of ideas for your own personal selection. But don't stop with our lists...the fun and the flavors should be yours!

# TIPS FROM OUR KIDS...

Hints from our kids are in two places in this book: In the "Baker says..." section for the individual recipe and in the Tips & Tools chapter. Pay attention to their first-hand experiences.

They can help you become a great baker, too!

# MEASURING...

Bread machines don't ask much of you, but they do require one thing — accuracy when measuring ingredients. Here's everything you need to know to conquer measuring and make great bread:

## WATER OR OTHER LIQUIDS...

Be certain to use a liquid measuring cup for water and other liquids. Measuring  cups for liquids are always clear, making it easy to see the liquid and the markings at the same time. Place the measuring cup on a level surface then fill the cup to the amount you need. Use lukewarm water. Cold water won't activate the yeast and very hot water may kill it. Double check the measurement, at eye level, to make sure the amount is exact.

## FLOUR...

Dry measuring cups are plastic or metal, but not clear. Select the exact cup size you need. (For example to measure 1/2 cup of flour you would use a 1/2 cup size cup, not a 3/4 cup.) Measure over the storage canister to keep excess flour out of the bread pan and off the counter or floor.

Stir flour and then gently spoon it into dry measuring cup. Overfill cup slightly, and then level off with the flat side of a table knife or flour leveler. **Do not** pack the flour into the measuring cup.

**1. Stir Flour and Spoon Into Cup**

**2. Overfill Slightly**

**3. Level Off With A Flat Edge**

# YEAST...

Yeast should be stored in the refrigerator, measured with a clean dry teaspoon, and leveled off with a flat edge.

# OTHER DRY INGREDIENTS...

White sugar, salt and other dry ingredients are also spooned gently into the right sized measuring tool and then gently leveled. The only exception to this rule is brown sugar — brown sugar is always packed into the measuring tool and then leveled. (If you have packed the brown sugar well, it will keep the shape of the measuring tool when it goes into the bread pan.)

# BUTTER...

We found our kids got the most accurate measurement using stick butter that had the measurements marked on the foil or paper wrapping. Set a table knife on the desired measurement and cut straight down along the marking. Be sure to unwrap the butter before placing it in the bread machine and to return the unused portion to the refrigerator for the next loaf. (Stick margarine may be substituted.)

# MEASURING SPOONS...

There are two sizes of measuring spoons — Tablespoons and teaspoons. They are not the same as spoons used for eating. These spoons are used to measure small amounts of both liquid and dry ingredients for baking. A Tablespoon holds 3 times as much as a teaspoon.

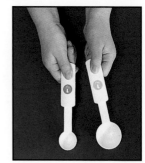

Sometimes our kids mixed up these two measuring spoons. To help you notice the difference, the word Tablespoon is capitalized throughout our book. Yeast is always measured in teaspoons. Here's a hint to remember which is the biggest: Try thinking of a table with a teapot on it. The <u>table</u> is always bigger than the <u>teapot</u> and the <u>Tablespoon</u> is always bigger than the <u>teaspoon</u>!

# BASIC DOUGH TECHNIQUES...

Our Family Favorites, Holiday Surprises and Let's Party pages show the detailed steps for making those breads. The dough secrets shown on the next four pages can be used to make all your dough handling easier and your finished breads terrific!

## FLOURING...

Always lightly flour your work surface and your rolling pin before you begin. Too much flour will cause the dough to slip on the surface and affect the taste. Too little flour will make it stick. A sprinkle of flour is the perfect place to start. Add more flour, a sprinkle at a time, if needed.

## THE DOUGH BALL...

When your machine has completed the dough cycle, dump the dough from the bread pan onto your lightly floured surface. If there are air bubbles in the dough, push on the dough to force the air bubbles out. Then shape the dough into a ball by turning it over and gently rotating it in a circle until the entire ball is lightly floured.

## ROLLING THE DOUGH...

When rolling out dough, don't use a back-and-forth motion. With a single sweep, push the dough in one direction...rolling the length of the dough and running off the edge. First push away, then pull toward yourself, then to each side. Repeat until the dough is the shape and size desired.

If the dough is too elastic (springs back) when you roll it, flip the dough over and continue rolling.

# DIVIDING THE DOUCH...

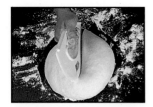

To divide your dough into equal pieces start with one of two basic shapes—a disc or a log. Make sure the disc or log is the same thickness all the way across before you start cutting.

Make the pieces equal in size each time you cut. The photos on each side show you how to divide into three, four, eight, or twelve pieces.

Our kids did best using a dough cutter with a rocking motion to cut.

# POUCH PINCH...

Our chef, Tim Doebler, showed us a great way to get a smooth ball every time. We've named it the "Pouch Pinch." Start with a piece of cut dough. Pull two sides up and pinch them together. Then take the two other sides and pull them up. Now pinch firmly in the middle to make the "pouch." Turn it over and the top will be round and smooth. Now roll the ball back and forth gently between the palms of your hands to finish the ball shape.

# OVEN BAKING TEMPERATURE AND TIME...

**Bake at 350° for 22-25 minutes**

Many breads are made from machine doughs and then baked in a conventional oven. This symbol tells you suggested oven baking temperature and approximate baking time. Preheat your oven to the temperature shown about 15 minutes before baking begins. Actual baking time will vary depending on how the dough was formed, kitchen temperature and your own oven. Check your project at the first time shown and continue checking every couple of minutes until done.

## PREPARING BAKING PANS...

Except for pizza, all of our dough breads are baked on a lightly greased baking sheet or pan. We like to use aerosol non-stick cooking spray. You can also apply margarine or shortening with a pastry brush and wipe with a paper towel.

## SEALING AND ATTACHING WITH WATER...

A dab of water works like magic to seal pieces of dough together or to attach one layer of dough to another. Simply dip your fingertip in a small bowl of water, dab the dough and then press firmly to seal.

## USING EGG WASH...

Egg wash adds a shiny finish to the bread crust. To make egg wash, break an egg into a small bowl or cup and stir with a fork until frothy. (An egg substitute product can also be used.)

Egg wash is applied with a pastry brush onto the shaped dough after rising and right before baking. Be sure to wash your hands after using raw egg.

## STORING AND FREEZING DOUGH...

Our test kitchen prepared lots of dough in advance for our kids to use. We found refrigerated dough was best when used within 12 hours. Frozen dough was best used within 4 weeks.

To store dough, remove from machine and make a dough ball. Spray the inside of a resealable plastic bag with non-stick cooking spray and place dough ball

inside. Force air from the bag, seal tightly, and store in your refrigerator or freezer.

When ready to use, let sit at room temperature until soft and pliable. (Refrigerated dough takes about one hour, while frozen dough takes two to three hours depending on the temperature of the room.)

Shape, let rise, and bake as usual.

# COLORING DOUGH...

Using colored dough is a lot of fun and it's easy. We use paste type food coloring (Page 169) instead of liquid food coloring because paste gives brighter colors. Food colors can stain, so be very careful. Color an entire batch or portions of a recipe by following the steps below.

**To color an entire batch:** Measure the water for the recipe. Then...

Get a small dab of color from the color paste jar.

Add color to water.

Stir until well mixed. Pour into bread pan.

Use this colored water instead of regular water, add the rest of the ingredients and select the dough cycle. That's it!

**To color a portion of a recipe:** Remove dough from the machine at the end of the dough cycle or first rise. Divide the dough into the number of pieces (2 to 5) you want to make into different colors. Then...

Place dough piece to be colored into bread pan.

Get a very small dab of paste color on knife.

Gently insert knife into dough to put in color.

Start machine.

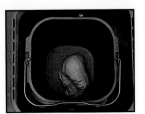

Knead until color is even. Stop machine.

Repeat with remaining pieces and colors. Be sure to thoroughly clean and dry the bread pan after each use. Depending on the recipe used, dough may need to be chilled for an hour to set color after mixing.

# SIMPLY DELICIOUS RECIPES

# WHITE BREAD

Calories 156 ◆ Cholesterol 6 mg. ◆ Sodium 296 mg. ◆ Protein 13% ◆ Carbohydrates 72% ◆ Fat 15%

Nutritional information per serving

## A

**Water**
1 + 1/4 cups

**White Bread Flour**
3 cups

**Dry Milk**
2 Tablespoons

**Sugar**
2 Tablespoons

**Salt**
1 + 1/2 teaspoons

**Butter**
2 Tablespoons

**Yeast**
fast rise
1 + 1/2 teaspoons
-or-
**Yeast**
active dry
2 teaspoons

## Molly says...

"I like to take the same kind of sandwich in my lunch just about every single day. I start the bread machine, using the timer, before I go to bed. Then in the morning, my Dad makes me a peanut butter and honey sandwich."

## B

**Water**
1 + 1/2 cups

**White Bread Flour**
4 cups

**Dry Milk**
3 Tablespoons

**Sugar**
3 Tablespoons

**Salt**
2 teaspoons

**Butter**
3 Tablespoons

**Yeast**
fast rise
2 teaspoons
-or-
**Yeast**
active dry
2 + 1/2 teaspoons

# DID YOU KNOW?????

To make Crumb Clay out of bread, remove crusts and then make the soft white part into fine crumbs. (⚠ A food processor makes this easy.) Mix 1 part white school glue with 4 parts bread crumbs. Work the mixture with your hands until it makes a soft, flexible dough. You can add details to your air-dried creations with fine-line markers.

Horse by Aly, age 7

# SWEET BREAD

Calories 169 ◆ Cholesterol 8 mg. ◆ Sodium 217 mg. ◆ Protein 13% ◆ Carbohydrates 67% ◆ Fat 20%
Nutritional information per serving

## A

**Water**
1 cup

**White Bread Flour**
3 cups

**Dry Milk**
2 Tablespoons

**Sugar**
3 Tablespoons

**Salt**
1 teaspoon

**Butter**
3 Tablespoons

**Yeast**
fast rise
1 teaspoon
-or-
**Yeast**
active dry
1 + 1/2 teaspoons

## Courtney
### says...

"Slices of this soft bread are very delicious with fruit and string cheese for lunch. I really like to make things out of this dough — especially cinnamon rolls!"

## B

**Water**
1 + 1/4 cups

**White Bread Flour**
4 cups

**Dry Milk**
3 Tablespoons

**Sugar**
1/4 cup

**Salt**
1 + 1/2 teaspoons

**Butter**
4 Tablespoons

**Yeast**
fast rise
1 + 1/2 teaspoons
-or-
**Yeast**
active dry
2 teaspoons

# DID YOU KNOW?????

**Pass the Bread, Please, Mummy....** The Egyptians were known in the ancient world as the "bread eaters." Egyptians were making yeast breads as early as 2600 B.C. (though it wasn't until more than 4,000 years later, when we started understanding chemistry, that anyone figured out how the process worked).

# GINGER BREAD

Calories 155 ◆ Cholesterol 3 mg. ◆ Sodium 200 mg.
Protein 14% ◆ Carbohydrates 74% ◆ Fat 12%
Nutritional information per serving

## A

**Water**
3/4 cup

**White Bread Flour**
3 cups

**Dry Milk**
1 Tablespoon

**Salt**
1 teaspoon

**Butter**
1 Tablespoon

**Cinnamon**
ground
1 teaspoon

**Ginger**
ground
1 teaspoon

**Nutmeg**
ground
1/2 teaspoon

**Cloves**
ground
1/2 teaspoon

**Molasses**
2 Tablespoons

**Large Egg**
1

**Yeast**
fast rise
1 + 1/2 teaspoons
-or-
**Yeast**
active dry
2 teaspoons

## Amy says...

"This bread reminds me of gingerbread cookies. I tell all my friends that it's great!"

• For tea parties, use cookie cutters to turn your bread slices into fancy shapes. Or, bake this dough in our form pans (Page 163). Decorate with fluffy white icing and your favorite jam.

## B

**Water**
1 cup

**White Bread Flour**
4 cups

**Dry Milk**
2 Tablespoons

**Salt**
1 + 1/2 teaspoons

**Butter**
2 Tablespoons

**Cinnamon**
ground
1 + 1/2 teaspoons

**Ginger**
ground
1 + 1/2 teaspoons

**Nutmeg**
ground
1 teaspoon

**Cloves**
ground
1 teaspoon

**Molasses**
3 Tablespoons

**Large Egg**
1

**Yeast**
fast rise
2 teaspoons
-or-
**Yeast**
active dry
2 + 1/2 teaspoons

# DID YOU KNOW??????

**Keeping In Touch By Eat-Mail...** In Germany, gingerbread makers were recognized as artists rather than cooks. Gingerbread was used for greeting cards beginning in the 1700's. Edible Christmas cards had gaily colored piped-sugar pictures of angels, doves, and other favorites. According to Bruce Cost, author of <u>Ginger East to West</u>, the German <u>lebkuchen</u> heart, became the most important lover's gift. It was baked with inscriptions and affixed with a small mirror. The practice of exchanging gingerbread hearts is still carried on in the former Yugoslavia.

# CHOCOLATE BREAD

Calories 145 ◆ Cholesterol 0 mg. ◆ Sodium 272 mg. ◆ Protein 13% ◆ Carbohydrates 82% ◆ Fat 6%

Nutritional information per serving

## A

**Water**
1 cup

**White Bread Flour**
3 cups

**Sugar**
3 Tablespoons

**Salt**
1 + 1/2 teaspoons

**Chocolate Chips**
large
1/4 cup

**Vanilla**
1/2 teaspoon

**Large Egg**
1

**Cocoa Powder**
1/4 cup

**Yeast**
fast rise
1 + 1/2 teaspoons
-or-
**Yeast**
active dry
2 teaspoons

## Matthew says...

"I make this bread the most because it tastes like real chocolate. That's it — what else is there to say? Chocolate is THE BEST!

P. S. It's really good with strawberry jam."

## B

**Water**
1 + 1/2 cups

**White Bread Flour**
4 cups

**Sugar**
1/4 cup

**Salt**
2 teaspoons

**Chocolate Chips**
large
1/2 cup

**Vanilla**
1 teaspoon

**Large Egg**
1

**Cocoa Powder**
1/2 cup

**Yeast**
fast rise
2 teaspoons
-or-
**Yeast**
active dry
3 teaspoons

**It Grows On Trees!** Chocolate is made from the seeds of the cacao (pronounced kuh-COW) fruit. There are about 30 - 40 of these white seeds, called cacao beans, in each yellow, green or red melon-shaped fruit. The beans are taken out of the fruit, fermented and dried. Then they are shipped to chocolate factories where they are roasted in large ovens to bring out the flavor. Then their hard skins are removed, and the beans are ground into a paste called chocolate liquor. Let the chocolate liquor harden and you have baking chocolate. But you can also separate the chocolate liquor into two separate ingredients — cocoa, and cocoa butter. When the chocolate liquor is mixed with extra cocoa butter and sugar, you get dark chocolate, or, if you add milk, milk chocolate. Though the ingredients are simple, the actual recipes are often closely guarded secrets.

# FRENCH BREAD

Calories 132 ◆ Cholesterol 0 mg. ◆ Sodium 271 mg. ◆ Protein 13% ◆ Carbohydrates 83% ◆ Fat 4%

Nutritional information per serving

## A

**Water**
1 + 1/4 cups

**White Bread Flour**
3 cups

**Sugar**
1 Tablespoon

**Salt**
1 + 1/2 teaspoons

**Yeast**
fast rise
1 + 1/2 teaspoons
**-or-**
**Yeast**
active dry
2 + 1/2 teaspoons

## Rosey says...

"This was the first bread I ever made in our bread machine. I liked it because I was five — and the recipe had five things in it. Then I showed my Grandpa how to make French bread. It was his first time to use a bread machine, too."

## B

**Water**
1 + 1/2 cups

**White Bread Flour**
4 cups

**Sugar**
2 Tablespoons

**Salt**
2 teaspoons

**Yeast**
fast rise
2 teaspoons
**-or-**
**Yeast**
active dry
3 teaspoons

**Waving Your Magic Baguette**... The traditional shape for French bread is the long "baguette," which is a French word meaning rod or wand. People often use a French bread baguette to make garlic bread by coating slices with a garlic and butter spread and broiling it in the oven.

# RAISIN BREAD

Calories 173 ◆ Cholesterol 6 mg. ◆ Sodium 318 mg. ◆ Protein 12% ◆ Carbohydrates 74% ◆ Fat 14%
Nutritional information per serving

## A

**Water**
1 + 1/4 cups

**White Bread Flour**
3 cups

**Dry Milk**
2 Tablespoons

**Sugar**
1 Tablespoon

**Salt**
1 + 1/2 teaspoons

**Butter**
2 Tablespoons

**Cinnamon**
1 teaspoon

**Raisins**
1/2 cup

**Yeast**
fast rise
1 + 1/2 teaspoons
-or-
**Yeast**
active dry
2 teaspoons

## Marisa
### says...

"Set your timer for warm bread in the morning, and your folks may let you sleep in a few minutes longer. You can fly out the door with a raisin bread and cream cheese breakfast sandwich."

• Even if you LOVE raisins, don't add extra when you make this recipe. Too much sugar from the extra fruit might spoil your loaf.

## B

**Water**
1 + 1/2 cups

**White Bread Flour**
4 cups

**Dry Milk**
2 Tablespoons

**Sugar**
2 Tablespoons

**Salt**
2 teaspoons

**Butter**
3 Tablespoons

**Cinnamon**
2 teaspoons

**Raisins**
1 cup

**Yeast**
fast rise
2 teaspoons
-or-
**Yeast**
active dry
2 + 1/2 teaspoons

# DID YOU KNOW?????

**Sorry, Mickey!** Keeping bread fresh has been a challenge through the ages. In castles, bread was sometimes stored in a huge wooden cradle. The bottom of the cradle was an open grate of wooden cross-pieces that kept air circulating around the bread to stop it from getting moldy. The cradle was suspended from the kitchen ceiling, and raised and lowered by ropes, which saved counter space and discouraged sampling by the kitchen mice.

# ORANGE PECAN BREAD

Calories 192 ◆ Cholesterol 6 mg. ◆ Sodium 208 mg. ◆ Protein 12% ◆ Carbohydrates 60% ◆ Fat 28%

Nutritional information per serving

## A

**Water**
1 + 1/4 cups

**White Bread Flour**
3 cups

**Dry Milk**
2 Tablespoons

**Salt**
1 teaspoon

**Butter**
2 Tablespoons

**Orange Peel**
1 + 1/2 Tablespoons

**Orange Marmalade**
3 Tablespoons

**Chopped Pecans**
1/2 cup

**Yeast**
fast rise
1 teaspoon
-or-
**Yeast**
active dry
1 + 1/2 teaspoons

## Corey
### says...

"This bread is great toasted. If you spread it with honey butter, it's almost like eating dessert."

## B

**Water**
1 + 1/2 cups

**White Bread Flour**
4 cups

**Dry Milk**
3 Tablespoons

**Salt**
1 + 1/2 teaspoons

**Butter**
3 Tablespoons

**Orange Peel**
2 Tablespoons

**Orange Marmalade**
1/4 cup

**Chopped Pecans**
1 cup

**Yeast**
fast rise
1 + 1/2 teaspoons
-or-
**Yeast**
active dry
2 teaspoons

# DID YOU KNOW??????

**Orange You Glad?** All forms of orange juice —
frozen concentrate, fresh squeezed or pasteur-
ized — contain the same proportion of vitamin C.
And orange juice retains up to 90 percent of its
vitamin C for up to 1 week if you store it in the
refrigerator. Frozen orange juice concentrate will
retain its vitamin C for up to a year if stored at 0° F
or lower.

43

# CHEESE BREAD

## A

**Water**
1 cup

**White Bread Flour**
3 cups

**Sugar**
1 Tablespoon

**Salt**
1 teaspoon

**Buttermilk**
powdered
1 Tablespoon

**Sour Cream**
1/4 cup

**Cheddar Cheese**
grated
1/2 cup

**Dried Chives**
1 Tablespoon

**Ranch Mix**
powdered
1 Tablespoon

**Yeast**
fast rise
1 teaspoon
**-or-**
**Yeast**
active dry
1 + 1/2 teaspoons

## B

**Water**
1 + 1/4 cups

**White Bread Flour**
4 cups

**Sugar**
2 Tablespoons

**Salt**
1 + 1/2 teaspoons

**Buttermilk**
powdered
2 Tablespoons

**Sour Cream**
1/2 cup

**Cheddar Cheese**
grated
1 cup

**Dried Chives**
2 Tablespoons

**Ranch Mix**
powdered
2 Tablespoons

**Yeast**
fast rise
1 teaspoon
**-or-**
**Yeast**
active dry
1 + 3/4 teaspoons

# Erin
## says...

"This bread smells fantastic and tastes even better. It has a secret ingredient — ranch dressing mix! Make this and your family will think you're a gourmet genius."

**Quick and Flat Breads...** The breads in this recipe book are all made with yeast, which makes the bread rise to give it a soft, chewy texture. There are two other main types of bread, which don't use yeast. One is "quick breads," which use baking powder or some other leavening agent to raise the dough. Muffins, biscuits, or corn bread are tasty examples. Another main type of bread is "flat breads." They have little or no leavening. These are made all over the world, and include tortillas, chapatis, pitas, and matzos.

DID YOU KNOW ?????

# GARLIC BREAD

Calories 145 ◆ Cholesterol 0 mg. ◆ Sodium 273 mg. ◆ Protein 12% ◆ Carbohydrates 76% ◆ Fat 12%
Nutritional information per serving

## A

**Water**
1 + 1/4 cups

**White Bread Flour**
3 cups

**Dry Milk**
1 Tablespoon

**Sugar**
1 Tablespoon

**Salt**
1 + 1/2 teaspoons

**Olive Oil**
1 Tablespoon

**Minced Garlic**
1 teaspoon

**Garlic Powder**
1 teaspoon

**Basil**
1/2 teaspoon

**Yeast**
fast rise
1 teaspoon
**-or-**
**Yeast**
active dry
1 + 1/2 teaspoons

## B

**Water**
1 + 1/2 cups

**White Bread Flour**
4 cups

**Dry Milk**
2 Tablespoons

**Sugar**
2 Tablespoons

**Salt**
2 teaspoons

**Olive Oil**
2 Tablespoons

**Minced Garlic**
1 + 1/2 teaspoons

**Garlic Powder**
1 + 1/2 teaspoons

**Basil**
1 teaspoon

**Yeast**
fast rise
1 + 1/2 teaspoons
**-or-**
**Yeast**
active dry
2 teaspoons

# Jayme
### says...

"I do love garlic bread! I especially like it with fettuccini alfredo and broccoli."

46

**A Healthy Smell...** People have known for ages that garlic is very good for us – and that it gives us garlic breath. Garlic has a chemical in it called sulfur. As you digest garlic, some of this sulfur enters your bloodstream. Then it's exhaled from your lungs, or it comes out of you when you sweat. According to Professor Eric Block, Ph.D., the human nose can detect less than one part of this sulfur in one billion parts of exhaled air. It has been reported that when mothers eat garlic shortly before giving birth, their babies are born with garlic breath.  But, lucky for them — other studies suggest that babies actually prefer slightly garlicky mother's milk. Parsley or orange will freshen your garlic breath.

DID YOU KNOW ????

# MOCHA BREAD

Calories 156 ◆ Cholesterol 21 mg. ◆ Sodium 295 mg. ◆ Protein 13% ◆ Carbohydrates 75% ◆ Fat 12%
Nutritional information per serving

## A

**Water**
1 cup

**White Bread Flour**
3 cups

**Dry Milk**
1 Tablespoon

**Sugar**
2 Tablespoons

**Salt**
1 + 1/2 teaspoons

**Butter**
1 Tablespoon

**Powdered Mocha Mix**
1/4 cup

**Large Egg**
1

**Yeast**
fast rise
1 teaspoon
**-or-**
**Yeast**
active dry
2 teaspoons

## Sarah
### says...

"Mocha Bread is really fluffy. I think it tastes good with peanut butter on it. It's a fabulous bread for a lazy morning."

## B

**Water**
1 + 1/4 cups

**White Bread Flour**
4 cups

**Dry Milk**
2 Tablespoons

**Sugar**
3 Tablespoons

**Salt**
2 teaspoons

**Butter**
2 Tablespoons

**Powdered Mocha Mix**
1/2 cup

**Large Egg**
1

**Yeast**
fast rise
1 + 1/4 teaspoons
**-or-**
**Yeast**
active dry
2 + 1/2 teaspoons

# DID YOU KNOW??????

**Mocha – It's Tres Sheik!** Most people nowadays think of "mocha" as a combination of coffee and chocolate flavors. It is also the name of a special kind of coffee originally imported from the Red Sea port of Mocha, in southwestern Arabia, in the country now known as Yemen.

# PIZZA BREAD

Calories 150 ◆ Cholesterol 2 mg. ◆ Sodium 278 mg.
Protein 15% ◆ Carbohydrates 73% ◆ Fat 12%
Nutritional information per serving

## A

**Water**
1 cup

**White Bread Flour**
3 cups

**Sugar**
1 Tablespoon

**Salt**
1 teaspoon

**Pizza Sauce**
2 Tablespoons

**Large Olives**
6 whole or sliced

**Parmesan**
grated
1 Tablespoon

**Dried Onions**
chopped
1 Tablespoon

**Pepperoni**
chopped
1/4 cup

**Mozzarella**
grated
3 Tablespoons

**Yeast**
fast rise
1 + 1/2  teaspoons
**-or-**
**Yeast**
active dry
1 + 1/2 teaspoons

Americans love
pizza. We eat more
Mozzarella than any
other cheese,
except Cheddar.

## Monica
### says...

"Pizza bread is almost a
meal in itself — two slices
and a salad is dinner for
me!"

## B

**Water**
1 + 1/4 cups

**White Bread Flour**
4 cups

**Sugar**
2 Tablespoons

**Salt**
2 teaspoons

**Pizza Sauce**
3 Tablespoons

**Large Olives**
8 whole or sliced

**Parmesan**
grated
2 Tablespoons

**Dried Onions**
chopped
2 Tablespoons

**Pepperoni**
chopped
1/2 cup

**Mozzarella**
grated
1/4 cup

**Yeast**
fast rise
1 + 1/2  teaspoons
**-or-**
**Yeast**
active dry
2 + 1/2 teaspoons

# DID YOU KNOW?????

**Buffalo Pizza, Anyone?** American Mozzarella is always made from cow's milk, but the original, Italian Mozzarella, is often made from water buffalo milk instead. In the 1940's, during World War II, as German Nazi soldiers were retreating from Italy, they destroyed all of the water buffalo. However, after the war, Italy brought in new water buffalo from India, so today there is a plentiful supply of <u>Mozzarella di bufala</u>.

# CINNAMON SUGAR BREAD

Calories 181 ◆ Cholesterol 11 mg. ◆ Sodium 319 mg. ◆ Protein 13% ◆ Carbohydrates 63% ◆ Fat 24%
Nutritional information per serving

## A

**Water**
1 cup

**White Bread Flour**
3 cups

**Sugar**
3 Tablespoons

**Salt**
1 + 1/2 teaspoons

**Butter**
1/4 cup

**Dry Milk**
3 Tablespoons

**Cinnamon**
2 + 1/2 teaspoons

**Yeast**
fast rise
1 + 1/2 teaspoons
-or-
**Yeast**
active dry
2 teaspoons

## Aly
### says...

"It's good! It's delicious! This looks like normal bread, but it smells and tastes like sugar and spice — a little bit of sugar, a little bit of cinnamon! And it's heavenly toasted!"

## B

**Water**
1 + 1/4 cups

**White Bread Flour**
4 cups

**Sugar**
1/4 cup

**Salt**
2 teaspoons

**Butter**
1/3 cup

**Dry Milk**
1/4 cup

**Cinnamon**
1 Tablespoon

**Yeast**
fast rise
2 teaspoons
-or-
**Yeast**
active dry
2 + 1/2 teaspoons

**Barking Up The Right Tree...** Cinnamon is the inner bark of a tropical evergreen tree. Cinnamon sticks, which are pieces of the curled bark, make great stirring sticks for hot drinks like cider and cocoa.

DID YOU KNOW?????

# BLUEBERRY BREAD

Calories 169 ◆ Cholesterol 6 mg. ◆ Sodium 318 mg. ◆ Protein 13% ◆ Carbohydrates 72% ◆ Fat 15%
Nutritional information per serving

## A

**Water**
1 + 1/4 cups

**White Bread Flour**
2 + 1/2 cups

**Wheat Bread Flour**
1/2 cup

**Dry Milk**
2 Tablespoons

**Salt**
1 + 1/2 teaspoons

**Butter**
2 Tablespoons

**Honey**
2 Tablespoons

**Blueberry Morning® Cereal**
1 cup

**Yeast**
fast rise
1 + 1/2 teaspoons
-or-
**Yeast**
active dry
2 teaspoons

## Kati
### says...

"I'm not much of a breakfast eater if I'm in a hurry. But vanilla yogurt with a couple of slices of this warm bread — that I can always make time for!"

## B

**Water**
1 + 1/2 cups

**White Bread Flour**
3 + 1/2 cups

**Wheat Bread Flour**
1/2 cup

**Dry Milk**
3 Tablespoons

**Salt**
2 teaspoons

**Butter**
3 Tablespoons

**Honey**
3 Tablespoons

**Blueberry Morning® Cereal**
1 + 1/4 cups

**Yeast**
fast rise
2 teaspoons
-or-
**Yeast**
active dry
2 + 1/2 teaspoons

**Feelin' Groovy...** For hundreds of years, millers ground flour using pairs of large "millstones" — a bedstone on the bottom that doesn't move, and a runner stone that turns above it. The grinding surfaces of these stones have "furrows," or grooves to spread the grain over the grinding surfaces and to keep the stones cool by ventilating them. Little marks called cracks or snecks were also carved into the surface for maximum grinding power. And do you know what? Some mills still stone-grind their flour today. Skilled craftsmen using special tools must work constantly to keep the millstones sharp, like it's been done for centuries.

# HONEY WHEAT BREAD

Calories 131 ◆ Cholesterol 3 mg. ◆ Sodium 194 mg. ◆ Protein 15% ◆ Carbohydrates 74% ◆ Fat 11%

Nutritional information per serving

## A

**Water**
1 + 1/4 cups

**White Bread Flour**
1 cup

**Wheat Bread Flour**
2 cups

**Dry Milk**
1 Tablespoon

**Brown Sugar**
1 Tablespoon

**Salt**
1 teaspoon

**Butter**
1 Tablespoon

**Honey**
1 Tablespoon

**Yeast**
fast rise
1 teaspoon
-or-
**Yeast**
active dry
2 teaspoons

## Sam
### says...

"This Honey Wheat Bread tastes really good, but it tastes even better with honey on top of it."

## B

**Water**
1 + 1/2 cups

**White Bread Flour**
1 cup

**Wheat Bread Flour**
3 cups

**Dry Milk**
2 Tablespoons

**Brown Sugar**
2 Tablespoons

**Salt**
1 + 1/2 teaspoons

**Butter**
2 Tablespoons

**Honey**
2 Tablespoons

**Yeast**
fast rise
1 + 1/2 teaspoons
-or-
**Yeast**
active dry
2 + 1/2 teaspoons

**Flour Power...** Farmers around the world grow over 18,000,000,000 (18 billion) bushels of wheat a year. Wheat covers more of the earth's surface than any other food crop. It takes about two square yards of land to produce enough flour to make a loaf of bread, and the average American eats over 125 pounds of flour annually. How many slices would your garden grow?

DID YOU KNOW ????

# TOASTED COCONUT BREAD

Calories 202 ◆ Cholesterol 6 mg. ◆ Sodium 318 mg. ◆ Protein 11% ◆ Carbohydrates 62% ◆ Fat 27%
Nutritional information per serving

## A

**Water**
1 cup

**White Bread Flour**
3 cups

**Dry Milk**
1 Tablespoon

**Sugar**
3 Tablespoons

**Salt**
1 + 1/2 teaspoons

**Butter**
2 Tablespoons

**Toasted Coconut**
1 cup

**Pure Coconut Milk**
1/4 cup

**Yeast**
fast rise
1 teaspoon
-or-
**Yeast**
active dry
2 teaspoons

## Michael says...

"The toasted coconut tastes so good, I like to make a little extra to eat as a snack while the loaf is baking!"

• To make toasted coconut, spread shredded coconut in an even layer on a baking sheet. ⚠ Toast it at 375° for about 15 minutes or until it turns golden brown. Cool before adding it to your bread machine, because too much heat kills the yeast!

## B

**Water**
1 + 1/4 cups

**White Bread Flour**
4 cups

**Dry Milk**
2 Tablespoons

**Sugar**
1/4 cup

**Salt**
2 teaspoons

**Butter**
3 Tablespoons

**Toasted Coconut**
1 + 1/2 cups

**Pure Coconut Milk**
1/2 cup

**Yeast**
fast rise
1 + 1/2 teaspoons
-or-
**Yeast**
active dry
2 + 1/4 teaspoons

# DID YOU KNOW?????

**So, Does This Mean Coconuts Aren't Mammals?**
The sweet, rich "coconut milk" used in this recipe has never seen the inside of a cow, so don't look for it in your dairy section. And "coconut milk" is not the liquid inside the coconut. Instead, it's this liquid blended with the "meat" of the coconut. It can be found in your grocer's Asian food section.

# 100% WHOLE WHEAT

Calories 137 ◆ Cholesterol 6 mg. ◆ Sodium 316 mg. ◆ Protein 16% ◆ Carbohydrates 68% ◆ Fat 16%

Nutritional information per serving

## A

**Water**
1 + 1/4 cups

**Wheat Bread Flour**
3 cups

**Dry Milk**
1 Tablespoon

**Brown Sugar**
2 Tablespoons

**Salt**
1 + 1/2 teaspoons

**Butter**
2 Tablespoons

**Molasses**
1 Tablespoon

**Gluten**
1 + 1/2 Tablespoons

**Yeast**
fast rise
1 teaspoon
-or-
**Yeast**
active dry
1 + 1/2 teaspoons

## Andrew
### says...

"I'm really active. I play basketball all winter and mountain bike and play soccer in the summer. As a vegetarian, I need my bread to pack plenty of nutrition. I like plain wheat bread sandwiches, with cheese and lettuce."

## B

**Water**
1 + 1/2 cups

**Wheat Bread Flour**
4 cups

**Dry Milk**
2 Tablespoons

**Brown Sugar**
3 Tablespoons

**Salt**
2 teaspoons

**Butter**
3 Tablespoons

**Molasses**
2 Tablespoons

**Gluten**
2 Tablespoons

**Yeast**
fast rise
1 + 1/2 teaspoons
-or-
**Yeast**
active dry
2 teaspoons

# DID YOU KNOW??????

**Food Fit For A King!** In the Middle Ages after King Arthur's time, the well-to-do often ate their food off squares of coarse whole grain bread, called trenchers, which they used like plates. When the meal was over, the diners would give their trenchers, still soaked with gravy or cream, to the poor to eat. For many hundreds of years, whole grain bread was only for the poor. The rich could afford refined white bread, and foolishly thought it was better. Nowadays more and more people eat whole grain bread, knowing it is a healthier food.

# MULTIGRAIN BREAD

Calories 165 ◆ Cholesterol 6 mg. ◆ Sodium 301 mg. ◆ Protein 14% ◆ Carbohydrates 71% ◆ Fat 15%
Nutritional information per serving

## A

**Water**
1 + 1/4 cups

**White Bread Flour**
2 + 1/4 cups

**Wheat Bread Flour**
1 cup

**Dry Milk**
1 Tablespoon

**Sugar**
2 Tablespoons

**Salt**
1 + 1/2 teaspoons

**Butter**
2 Tablespoons

**7 Grain Cereal**
1/4 cup

**Cracked Wheat**
1 Tablespoon

**Yeast**
fast rise
1 teaspoon
**-or-**
**Yeast**
active dry
2 teaspoons

## Nyaling
### says...

"My Mother is always trying to get me to eat healthy stuff. I wish it all tasted as good as this bread!"

## B

**Water**
1 + 1/2 cups

**White Bread Flour**
2 + 1/2 cups

**Wheat Bread Flour**
1 cup

**Dry Milk**
2 Tablespoons

**Sugar**
3 Tablespoons

**Salt**
2 teaspoons

**Butter**
3 Tablespoons

**7 Grain Cereal**
1/2 cup

**Cracked Wheat**
2 Tablespoons

**Yeast**
fast rise
1 + 1/2 teaspoons
**-or-**
**Yeast**
active dry
2 + 1/2 teaspoons

# DID YOU KNOW?????

**Bite Into Billions...** A key ingredient for bread is yeast, which is a microscopic fungus. These individual living cells are so tiny that it takes 20,000,000,000 (20 billion) of them to weigh one gram — about the weight of two regular **m&m's**®.

# RYE BREAD

Calories 155 ◆ Cholesterol 6 mg. ◆ Sodium 202 mg. ◆ Protein 12% ◆ Carbohydrates 72% ◆ Fat 16%

Nutritional information per serving

## A

**Water**
1 + 1/4 cups

**White Bread Flour**
2 + 1/2 cups

**Brown Sugar**
2 Tablespoons

**Salt**
1 teaspoon

**Butter**
2 Tablespoons

**Rye Flour**
3/4 cup

**Whole Caraway Seeds**
2 teaspoons

**Yeast**
fast rise
1 teaspoon
-or-
**Yeast**
active dry
1 + 1/2 teaspoons

## Martin
### says...

"When my friend Elan first tasted this bread he said, 'Pastrami, NOW! Quick! I want some pastrami and a couple of those big deli pickles!' "

## B

**Water**
1 + 1/2 cups

**White Bread Flour**
3 cups

**Brown Sugar**
3 Tablespoons

**Salt**
2 teaspoons

**Butter**
3 Tablespoons

**Rye Flour**
1 cup

**Whole Caraway Seeds**
1 Tablespoon

**Yeast**
fast rise
1 + 1/4 teaspoons
-or-
**Yeast**
active dry
2 teaspoons

# DID YOU KNOW?????

**This Is A Stick-up!** Gluten is a sticky, stretchy protein found in some grains. When yeast ferments with natural sugars in the flour's starch, or with added sugar, it produces bubbles of carbon dioxide gas. The sticky gluten forms walls around these gas bubbles, and gives the bread its shape as it rises. Rye flour is high in protein, but low in gluten. If you only used rye flour, you would have very heavy bread that would not rise on its own. As a result, no more than 20 - 30% of the flour in a bread can be rye; the rest usually needs to be wheat flour, which has a high gluten content. Some grains, like corn, barley and oats, have no gluten.

# OATMEAL BREAD

Calories 164 ◆ Cholesterol 6 mg. ◆ Sodium 295 mg. ◆ Protein 13% ◆ Carbohydrates 70% ◆ Fat 17%
Nutritional information per serving

## A

**Water**
1 cup

**White Bread Flour**
2 + 1/2 cups

**Dry Milk**
1 + 1/2 Tablespoons

**Brown Sugar**
3 Tablespoons

**Salt**
1 + 1/2 teaspoons

**Butter**
2 Tablespoons

**Oats**
1/2 cup

**Yeast**
fast rise
2 teaspoons
-or-
**Yeast**
active dry
2 + 1/2 teaspoons

## Jamie
### says...

"My favorite breakfast is scrambled eggs, bacon and orange juice with oatmeal bread, toasted with strawberry jam!"

• You can use either quick or old fashioned oats.

## B

**Water**
1 + 1/4 cups

**White Bread Flour**
3 cups

**Dry Milk**
2 Tablespoons

**Brown Sugar**
1/4 cup

**Salt**
2 teaspoons

**Butter**
3 Tablespoons

**Oats**
1 cup

**Yeast**
fast rise
2 + 1/2 teaspoons
-or-
**Yeast**
active dry
3 teaspoons

**Peanut Butter & Jelly Montague, Anyone?** You probably know that the "sandwich" is named after a British lord whose title was "4th Earl of Sandwich." But did you know his name was John Montague? What if he had lived in America, where we don't have titles? Do you think we'd be eating grilled cheese montagues, baloney montagues, and toasted tuna montagues? The sandwich got its name in 1762, when Montague spent 24 hours at a gaming table, without stopping to take food other than pieces of meat that were brought to him between two slices of bread.

DID YOU KNOW ????

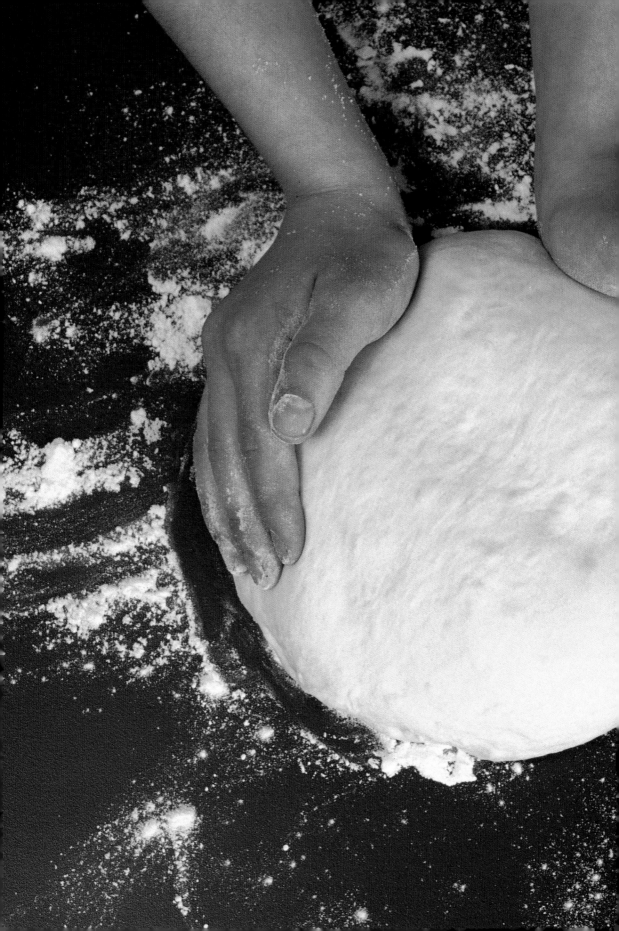

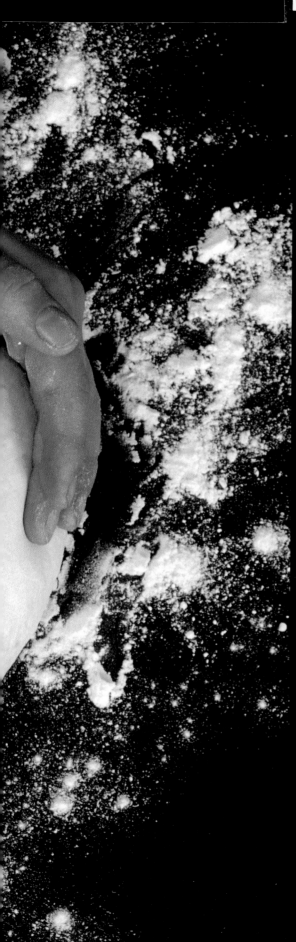

# FUN
# FAMILY
# FAVORITES

**TOOLS:** rolling pin, pizza cutter, two baking sheets, pastry brush, small bowl

# PRETZELS

This is a great dough to make in advance and keep in your fridge. Roll 'em, twist 'em, bake 'em and eat 'em when school is out or friends come over.

Bake at 375° for 15-18 minutes

## DOUGH RECIPE

**Water**
1 cup

**White Bread Flour**
3 cups

**Sugar**
1/4 cup

**Salt**
1 teaspoon

**Butter**
2 Tablespoons

**Yeast**
fast rise
2 teaspoons
**-or-**
**Yeast**
active dry
3 teaspoons

## Pretzel Wash:

**1 Egg**
beaten

**White Vinegar**
2 Tablespoons

Beat together with fork until very well mixed.

## Topping:

**Kosher Salt**
2 Tablespoons

# Cale
## says...

"My soccer team loves these pretzels for an after-game snack – win or lose!"

70

**1.**
Place dough on lightly floured surface. Roll dough into an 8–inch by 16–inch rectangle.

**2.**
Use pizza cutter to cut into long, narrow strips about 3/4–inch wide.

**3.**
Bend one strip into a "horseshoe."

**4.**
Cross your hands, picking up one end of the strip with each hand.

**5.**
Uncross your hands, placing the dough into the pretzel shape.

**6.**
Lift one end at a time, and dab a bit of water to connect the top strip ends to the bottom layer.

**7.** Repeat with every strip and put on lightly greased baking sheets.

**8.** Let rise for 1 hour or until double in size. Preheat oven to 375°.

**9.**
Brush with "Pretzel Wash."

**10.** Sprinkle with kosher salt.

**11.** ⚠ Bake until golden brown, about 15 to 18 minutes.

**TOOLS:** Rolling pin, pastry brush or small spatula, small bowl of water, dough cutter 9-inch by 13-inch baking pan, small resealable plastic bag, scissors

# CINNAMON ROLLS

Bake at 350° for 30-35 minutes

## Molly says...

"I've baked these from Anchorage to New York City and they are a hit in every town!"

• If you love lots of icing, spread it onto the rolls right from the can.

### DOUGH RECIPE

**Water**
1 cup

**White Bread Flour**
3 cups

**Dry Milk**
2 Tablespoons

**Sugar**
3 Tablespoons

**Salt**
1 teaspoon

**Butter**
3 Tablespoons

**Yeast**
fast rise
1 teaspoon
**-or-**
**Yeast**
active dry
1 + 1/2 teaspoons

### FILLING:

**Soft Butter**
1/2 cup

**Sugar**
1/2 cup

**Cinnamon**
3 Tablespoons

### OPTIONAL FILLINGS:

**Raisins**
1/2 cup

**Chopped Nuts**
1/2 cup

### Topping:

**White Icing**
1 can

BREAD

**1.**

Roll dough into a 12-inch by 18-inch rectangle on lightly floured work surface.

**2.**

Spread soft butter over the top of the dough with pastry brush or small spatula.

**3.**

Sprinkle sugar on top of butter. Then shake on the cinnamon. Add raisins and nuts if you wish.

**4.**

Tightly roll dough from the bottom to the top.

**5.**

Wet edge and pinch firmly to seal filling inside.

**6.**

Cut dough roll into twelve equal slices. Be careful to not squish the log while cutting.

**7.**

Lay the rolls cut-side up into the lightly greased pan. Cover and let rise until double in size, about one hour. Preheat oven to 350°.

**8.**

⚠ Bake, about 30 to 35 minutes. While cinnamon rolls are cooling, spoon icing into a self-sealing plastic bag. Remove air and seal bag. Twist the top to push the icing into one corner of the bag. Snip a tiny corner off the bag.

**9.**

Squeeze icing on top of the cinnamon rolls.

**TOOLS:** dough cutter, small bowl of water, baking sheet, egg wash, pastry brush

# BRAIDED BREAD

**DOUGH**

**Baker's Choice**

**White** (Page 30)
**Cheese** (Page 44)
**French** (Page 38)
**Honey Wheat**
(Page 56)

**Seed Toppings:**

**Poppy Seed**
**Sesame Seed**

You can divide your dough into as many equally-sized pieces as you would like to have ropes in your braid. Cale made a 5-strand, Kyle a 7-strand, and Kelsey impressed us all with a double batch, two-layered braid.

**Bake at 350° for 35-40 minutes**

## Kelsey says...

"Place the ropes close and wrap them tightly together, to be sure your braid is strong and beautiful."

• For that special breakfast or Sunday brunch, make two multi-flavored braids using batches of Sweet (Page 32) and Chocolate (Page 36) dough.

multicolored
(Circus Braids Page 120)

5-color braid

**1.**

On lightly floured work surface, divide dough into three equal pieces. (Braiding steps shown in color to make it easy to follow.)

**2.**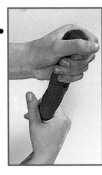

Roll each piece into an 18-inch rope. Hold one end up and gently squeeze your way down the dough, using gravity to help you make the rope longer.

**3.**

Roll back and forth on the work surface starting in the center and working to the end, to get a smooth rope.

**4.**

Wet fingers and tightly pinch all three ropes together at one end.

**5.**

Lift the left outside rope and move it to the middle, between the other two ropes.

**6.**

Lift the right outside rope and move it to the middle.

**7.**

Continue moving the outside ropes to the middle, alternating the left side and right side, until the braid is done.

**8.**

Pinch and seal the three ropes together with a dab of water. Tuck the ends underneath.

**9.**

Lay braid on lightly greased baking sheet. Cover and let rise about 1 hour or until double in size. Preheat oven to 350°

**10.** Brush with egg wash and sprinkle with seeds, if desired. ⚠ Bake until golden brown, about 35 to 40 minutes.

**11.** ⚠ Remove to cooling rack. Cool before slicing.

finished braid

**TOOLS:** dough cutter, baking sheet, egg wash, pastry brush, paring knife

# SOUP BOWLS

Serve these filled with thick, creamy soups or chili – and you can even eat the dishes!

Bake at 375° for 25-28 minutes

## DOUGH RECIPE

**Water**
1 + 1/4 cups

**White Bread Flour**
3 cups

**Dry Milk**
2 Tablespoons

**Sugar**
2 Tablespoons

**Salt**
1 + 1/2 teaspoons

**Butter**
2 Tablespoons

**Yeast**
fast rise
1 + 1/2 teaspoons
-or-
**Yeast**
active dry
2 teaspoons

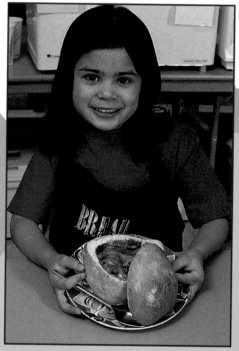

## Quinsey says...

"I need to be very gentle with my dough, so I like to pretend I'm handling a little baby kitten."

- When putting the dough pieces on the baking sheet, place the pieces with a cut-side down for a nice, flat bottom.

- Use the bread crumbs from the inside of the bowls to feed the birds or to make Crumb Clay (Page 26).

**1.**  On a lightly floured surface, cut dough into four equal pieces.

**2.**  Set each piece with one of the cut sides down. Gently round each piece between your hands forming a nice ball.

**3.**  Place onto a greased baking sheet. Very gently round the tops with the palm of your hand. Cover and let rise in a warm spot for about an hour, until double in size. Preheat oven to 375°.

**4.**  Lightly brush tops and sides of the bowls with egg wash.

**5.** ⚠ Place in oven to bake, about 25 to 28 minutes. ⚠ When done, remove from baking sheet to wire rack and cool completely.

**6.**  ⚠ Use a sharp knife to cut a circle "lid" from the top of each bowl. Save the lids for serving.

**7.**  Pull out the soft bread, hollowing the soup bowl like a pumpkin. Leave thick sides and bottom so your bowl doesn't leak.

**TOOLS:** dough cutter, rolling pin, pizza cutter, scissors, small mixing bowl, 2 baking sheets, small bowl of water

# CHEESE PINWHEELS

Bake at 375° for 15-18 minutes

## DOUGH RECIPE

**Water**
1/4 cup

**White Bread Flour**
3 cups

**Sugar**
2 Tablespoons

**Salt**
1 + 1/2 teaspoons

**Butter**
3 Tablespoons

**Tomato Juice**
1/2 cup

**Cheddar Cheese**
1/2 cup
grated

**Yeast**
fast rise
1 + 1/2 teaspoons
-or-
**Yeast**
active dry
2 teaspoons

## FILLING:

**Cheddar Cheese**
2 cups
grated

**Chives**
3 Tablespoons
chopped

Gently mix together in a small bowl.

## Justin says...

"I like this cheesy flavor. These are a great snack for after my friends and I have been bike riding around the neighborhood."

• Rosey and Molly made tiny pinwheels for a doll's tea party. As long as you start with a square, this dough technique will work for any size pinwheel.

• Use 1/3 of the dough to make 6 breadsticks. Attach a pinwheel to the breadstick handle with a frilled toothpick. Use as a fun party favor or summer lunchtime treat!

78

**1.**

Divide the dough in half on lightly floured work surface.

**2.**

Roll one of the halves into an 8-inch by 12-inch rectangle.

**3.**

Cut into six 4-inch by 4-inch squares.

**4.**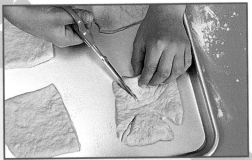

Lay each square onto a lightly greased baking sheet. Use scissors to cut a slit from each corner of the square ALMOST, but not quite, to the middle.

**5.**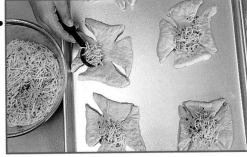

Sprinkle 2 Tablespoons of the cheese/chive filling onto the center of each square.

**6.**

To make a pinwheel, LIFT one corner of the square and press it firmly to the center. SKIP the next corner. Continue to LIFT one, SKIP one, all around the pinwheel. Seal by dabbing water between the dough layers and pressing down firmly on the center.

**7.** Repeat with the remaining dough. Add a light sprinkling of cheese on the finished pinwheels. Preheat oven to 375°.

**8.** Let rise 10 minutes. ⚠ Bake, about 15 to 18 minutes. Delicious warm!

**TOOLS:** dough cutter, rolling pin, small bowl of water, fork, baking sheet

# LUNCH POCKETS

Bake at 350° for 25-30 minutes

## DOUGH RECIPE

**Baker's Choice!**

**White**
(Page 30)

**Cheese**
(Page 44)

**Garlic**
(Page 46)

**Multi-Grain**
(Page 62)

**Rye**
(Page 64)

## FILLING IDEAS

**Baker's Choice!**

- ham
- pepperoni
- grated cheese
- olives
- diced onion
- finely chopped veggies
- peanut butter and jelly...

## Sarah says...

"I made these with garlic bread dough because it's one of my favorites. My friends came up with all kinds of combinations of doughs and fillings. They even changed 'lunch pockets' to 'brunch pockets' by using chocolate dough with a cream cheese and raspberry jam filling."

- As with any other food made with meat, eggs or cheese, refrigerate leftovers.

**1.**  Make the dough of your choice. Preheat oven to 350°. Cut dough in half on lightly floured work surface.

**2.** 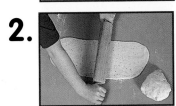 Roll one of the halves into an 8-inch by 16-inch rectangle.

**3.** 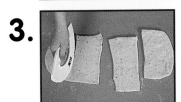 Cut the rectangle into four pieces, each about 4 inches by 8 inches.

**4.**  Add your favorite filling to one end of each rectangle.

**5.**  Fold dough over the fillings. Dab the inside edges with water and seal.

**6.**  Press the outer edges together with a fork. You can also press with your fingertips, but make sure you seal completely, so the filling doesn't leak out.

**7.** Repeat with remaining dough.

**8.**  Decorate the outside of the Lunch Pockets with a dough letter, a piece of filling, or a shape to remind you which fillings you put inside.

**9.** ⚠ Bake until golden brown, about 25 to 30 minutes.

**TOOLS:** rolling pin, ruler, rubber spatula, dough cutter, 2 baking sheets, 2 mixing bowls, wire whisk

# PEANUT TWISTERS

Bake at 350° for 15-18 minutes

## FILLING:

**Peanut Butter**
1/2 cup

**Powdered Sugar**
1/4 cup

**Soft Butter**
3 Tablespoons

Mix together until smooth.

## Topping:

**Powdered Sugar**
1 cup

**Water**
3 Tablespoons

**Soft Butter**
2 Tablespoons

**Cocoa Powder**
2 Tablespoons

Mix together until smooth.

## DOUGH RECIPE

**Water**
1 cup

**White Bread Flour**
3 cups

**Dry Milk**
3 Tablespoons

**Sugar**
1/4 cup

**Salt**
1 + 1/2 teaspoons

**Butter**
1/4 cup

**Yeast**
fast rise
1 + 1/2 teaspoons
**-or-**
**Yeast**
active dry
2 teaspoons

# Martin says...

"These taste just like Reese's® Peanut Butter Cups — but I can eat them for breakfast!"

• If you are the "crunchy type," use chunky peanut butter or, better yet, sprinkle 1/2 cup of chopped peanuts over the filling before you fold the dough.

**1.**  Roll dough into a 12-inch by 16-inch rectangle on lightly floured work surface.

**2.**  Mix filling in small bowl and spread a thin layer over the rectangle.

**3.** 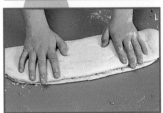 Slide your hands under one side of dough, lift and carefully fold in half.

**4.**  Use dough cutter to cut into 16 strips. Each strip should be about one inch wide. Lightly grease the baking sheets.

**5.**  Pick up one end of a strip in each hand. Give the strip several twists.

**6.**  Press both ends of the Twister firmly onto the baking sheet to keep it from untwisting. Preheat oven to 350°.

**7.** Let rise 20 minutes. ⚠ Bake until golden brown, about 15 to 18 minutes.

**8.**  While Twisters are baking, make chocolate topping. ⚠ When Twisters are slightly cooled, drizzle chocolate topping over them.

**TOOLS:** 9-inch by 13-inch baking pan, dough cutter

# SAVORY BREADSTICKS

Bake at 400° for 15-18 minutes

These are so soft, warm and full of flavor we were tempted to call them dinner rolls instead of breadsticks.

## Other Things You'll Need:

**Butter**
1/2 cup

**Parmesan Cheese**
1/2 cup
grated

## DOUGH RECIPE

**Water**
1 + 1/4 cups

**White Bread Flour**
3 cups

**Dry Milk**
2 Tablespoons

**Sugar**
2 Tablespoons

**Salt**
1 + 1/2 teaspoons

**Butter**
2 Tablespoons

**Yeast**
fast rise
1 + 1/2 teaspoons
-or-
**Yeast**
active dry
2 teaspoons

## Matthew says...

"Because these are so easy, I like to make them after school to go with our family's dinner."

• Sprinkle with sesame seeds before baking to add extra nutrition and flavor!

**1.**  ⚠ With grown-up help, melt 1/2 cup butter in baking pan. Set aside to cool.

**2.**  On lightly floured work surface, divide dough into 12 equal pieces.

**3.**  Roll each dough piece into a rope about 13 inches long. Lay the ropes side by side in baking pan.

**4.**  Sprinkle cheese over the top of the breadsticks.

**5.** Cover and let rise 30 minutes. Preheat oven to 400°.

**6.** ⚠ Bake until golden brown, about 15 to 18 minutes. Serve in pan while still warm.

**It's A Matter Of Taste...** Savory can mean tasty, but it's also a word cooks use to refer to something that's not sweet. Unfortunately, some people don't have the ability to taste, and others don't have the ability to smell. There are names for these conditions. Do you know what they are? They are much less common than the words for an inability to see (blindness) or hear (deafness). When people lack their sense of smell, it's called anosmia, from Greek words "an" (without) and "osme" (smell). It's pretty uncommon. It's even more rare if someone has "ageusia" or "ageustia," which means a loss of the sense of taste. These come from Greek and Latin words for taste.

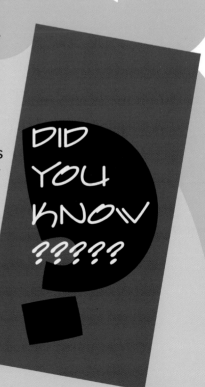

DID YOU KNOW ?????

**TOOLS:** dough cutter, rolling pin, large spoon, small bowl of water, baking sheet

# EGG IN AN EGG

Bake at 375° for 20-22 minutes

## FILLINGS:
• 6 Eggs
⚠ Scrambled and seasoned to taste

## Baker's Choice:
• grated cheese
• salsa
• chopped ham
• bacon bits...

## DOUGH RECIPE

**Water**
1 + 1/4 cups

**White Bread Flour**
3 cups

**Dry Milk**
2 Tablespoons

**Sugar**
2 Tablespoons

**Salt**
1 + 1/2 teaspoons

**Butter**
2 Tablespoons

**Yeast**
fast rise
1 + 1/2 teaspoons
**-or-**
**Yeast**
active dry
2 teaspoons

# Kyle says...

"I invented these one day when I got hungry while we were baking in the Test Kitchen."

• ⚠ Always wash your hands thoroughly after handling eggs.

• For an extra-delicious crust, ⚠ brush with butter right after you take them out of the oven.

• Make these the night before, store in refrigerator and reheat the next morning for an easy "breakfast-to-go."

**1.**  ⚠ Scramble eggs and set aside. On lightly floured work surface, cut dough in four equal pieces.

**2.**  Roll or pat each piece into a 6-inch circle. Spoon scrambled eggs onto the center of each piece.

**3.**  Add whatever other breakfast fillings you like.

**4.**  Using the "Pouch Pinch" (Page 25), stretch the sides of the dough up around the fillings. Pinch well to seal tightly.

**5.**  Turn seam side down and gently form an oval "egg" shape between your hands. Preheat oven to 375°.

**6.** Let rise 10 minutes. ⚠ Bake until golden brown, about 20 to 22 minutes. Let cool slightly and enjoy! Refrigerate leftovers.

**TOOLS:** 2 bowls, Bundt® pan or standard loaf pan

# SWEET PULLAPARTS

Bake at 350°
for 40-50
minutes

## DOUGH RECIPE

**Water**
1 cup

**White Bread Flour**
3 cups

**Dry Milk**
2 Tablespoons

**Sugar**
3 Tablespoons

**Salt**
1 teaspoon

**Butter**
3 Tablespoons

**Yeast**
fast rise
1 teaspoon
**-or-**
**Yeast**
active dry
1 + 1/2 teaspoons

## Other Things You'll Need:

**Butter**
1/2 cup

⚠ Melt and set aside.

**Sugar**
1 cup

**Cinnamon**
3 Tablespoons

Mix the cinnamon and sugar together in a bowl and set aside.

## Tiana says...

"These are best warm right from the oven with a tall glass of cold milk. Grab a piece and pull it off!"

• If you don't have a Bundt pan, use a standard loaf pan instead and bake for about 35-45 minutes. It will look different, but taste just as good.

88

**1.**   Place dough on lightly floured work surface. Pull off pieces about the size of a ping pong ball, one after another, until all the dough is used.

**2.**  Gently roll each piece into a ball with the palms of your hands.

**3.**  Roll all dough balls in the melted butter and set aside. Then roll the buttered balls in the cinnamon sugar mixture and arrange in the bottom of the pan.

**4.**  Evenly layer in the baking pan, piling the balls gently on top of each other.

**5.**  Cover and let rise until double in size, about one hour. Preheat oven to 350°.

**6.** ⚠ Bake, about 40 to 50 minutes. ⚠ Remove from oven and cool in pan briefly, about 5 minutes.

**7.** ⚠ Have an adult turn the pan upside down onto a serving plate.

**TOOLS:** dough cutter, baking sheet, egg wash, pastry brush, scissors

# BASIC DINNER ROLLS

Bake at 375° for 20-25 minutes

## DOUGH

### Baker's Choice

These rolls are great with about any kind of bread dough you make. White, Honey Wheat, Cheese, or Garlic...also add your choice of seed toppings (no bird seed please)!

**1.**

On lightly floured work surface, divide dough into twelve equal pieces.

**2.**

Use the "Pouch Pinch" (Page 25) to shape each dough piece. Turn over and gently roll the dough ball between your palms to make a smooth, rounded roll. Place onto a lightly greased baking sheet.

**3.**

Lightly brush rolls with egg wash. Make two snips on the top of each roll with a scissors. Sprinkle the roll with your favorite seed topping. Repeat with remaining dough pieces.

**4.**

Cover and let rise until doubled in size, about an hour. Preheat oven to 375°.

For a softer crust, Courtney baked her dinner rolls in an 8–inch by 8–inch pan. Instead of seeds, she brushed her rolls with butter while still warm.

**5.** ⚠ Bake until golden brown, about 20 to 25 minutes.

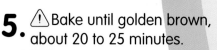

**TOOLS:** rolling pin, dough cutter, small bowl, pastry brush, baking sheet

# CRESCENT ROLLS

Bake at 375° for 18-20 minutes

### What You'll Need:
1 batch White Bread dough
1/2 cup melted butter

**1.**

Cut dough in half on lightly floured work surface.

**2.**

Shape each half into a nice round ball by rolling it gently between the palms of your hands.

**3.**

Roll each ball into a 12–inch circle. Brush circle lightly with melted butter.

**4.**

Make three cuts all the way across the circle to create 6 pie–shaped wedges.

**5.**

Beginning at the wide end, roll each wedge up to the pointed tip.

**6.**

Lay the rolls on the baking sheet with the tip side down. Curve the ends slightly and press down onto pan.

**7.** Let rise until double in size, about one hour. Preheat oven to 375°.

**8.** ⚠ Bake until golden brown, about 18 to 20 minutes.

**9.** Brush tops with butter while still warm.

This bunny hopped over from Page 122.

**TOOLS:** dough cutter, two six-muffin pans, small bowl, pastry brush

# CLOVERLEAF ROLLS

Bake at 375° for 20-25 minutes

## Baker's Choice

Like Basic Dinner Rolls, these are great with any kind of bread dough you choose.

**1.**  On a lightly floured work surface, cut dough into 36 pieces, all about the same size.

**2.** Gently roll each piece into a ball between the palms of your hands.

**3.**  Place three balls into each muffin cup. Repeat until all muffin cups are filled, for a total of 12 rolls.

For St. Patrick's Day, Jayme, Courtney and Amy used green dough (Page 27) to make these Irish shamrock dinner rolls.

**4.** Cover and let rise until double in size, about an hour. Preheat oven to 375°.

**5.** ⚠ Bake until golden brown, about 20-25 minutes.

**6.**  ⚠ Brush tops with melted butter while rolls are still warm.

**TOOLS:** dough cutter, 9-inch round pan, small bowl, pastry brush

# APRIL FOOL'S DAY

Bake at 375°
for 20-25
minutes

**FILLING IDEAS**

## Baker's Choice

- cheese cubes
- pecans
- olives
- halved caramels
- chocolate chips
- maraschino cherries

**1.**

On a lightly floured work surface, cut dough into 8 pieces.

**2.**

Pat a piece of dough into a circle and add the surprise of your choice.

**3.**

Use the "Pouch Pinch" (Page 25) to pull the dough around the surprise. Wet with water to seal. Turn dough piece over and roll gently between palms to form a smooth ball.

**4.**

Place formed roll into pan. Continue filling the remaining dough pieces with different sweet and savory surprises.

**5.** Cover and let rise until double in size, about 1 hour. Preheat oven to 375°.

**6.** ⚠ Bake until golden brown, about 20 to 25 minutes.

**7.**

For April Fool's Day, Galen tucked a small treat (or trick!) into each roll before he pinched them closed. What do you think Galen hid inside these rolls?

⚠ Brush tops with melted butter while rolls are still warm.

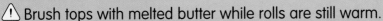

# HOLIDAY SURPRISES

**TOOLS:** dough cutter, small bowl of water, large baking sheet, plastic wrap, microwave, spoon

# LAST YEAR'S BREAD

Bake at 375°
for 20-25
minutes

## DOUGH

### Baker's Choice

- **Raisin** (Page 40)
- **Orange Pecan** (Page 42)
- **Blueberry** (Page 54)
- **Chocolate** (Page 36)

### Toppings:

- 1 can White Icing
- Crystal Sprinkles

You can make bread one year and eat it the next! Make this your New Year's Eve project, and on the first morning of the New Year, you'll be serving your family a scrumptious treat.

**Corey** says... "For a birthday breakfast celebration, make the bread dough into the numbers of the person's age!"

**1.**

Divide dough into four equal pieces on lightly floured work surface.

**2.**

Roll pieces into ropes long enough to form each numeral.

**3.**

Form each rope into one of the numerals of the new year. Wet ends and pinch firmly to seal.

**4.**

Lay numerals onto a lightly greased large baking sheet.

**5.** Cover with plastic wrap. Make sure the entire pan is air-tight. Put into refrigerator.

**6.** Next year (that is, the next morning!), remove from refrigerator. Let rise until double in size, about 2 hours. Preheat oven to 375°.

**7.** ⚠ Bake until golden brown, about 20 to 25 minutes. ⚠ Remove from oven and cool on wire rack.

**8.** ⚠ Open icing, removing all foil, and warm for 30 seconds in microwave. Use spoon to drizzle icing across the numerals and add sprinkles as shown in photo on the opposite page.

**TOOLS:** dough cutter, rolling pin, spoon, small bowl of water, baking sheet, cooling rack

# VALENTINE'S HEART

**Rosey says...**

"For my friends I make paper Valentines, but for my family I like to make a Valentine's Heart to eat!"

Bake at 350° for 25-30 minutes

## DOUGH RECIPE

**Water**
1 cup

**White Bread Flour**
3 cups

**Dry Milk**
2 Tablespoons

**Sugar**
3 Tablespoons

**Salt**
1 teaspoon

**Butter**
3 Tablespoons

**Yeast**
fast rise
1 teaspoon
-or-
**Yeast**
active dry
1 + 1/2 teaspoons

## FILLING:
**Cherry Pie Filling**
1 can

## Toppings:
**White Icing**
1 can

**Valentine Sprinkles**

- Use this same idea to make two candy cane breads in December! Place each side of the heart on a separate baking sheet. Shape into a candy cane. Before baking, use a pastry brush to paint on 'stripes' of egg wash, then sprinkle the wet stripes with red decorator sugar.

**1.**

Cut dough in half on lightly floured work surface.

**2.**

Roll one of the halves into a 6-inch by 18-inch rectangle.

**3.**

Spoon half of the cherries down the center of the rectangle. Scoop mostly cherries and not the extra sauce.

**4.**

Fold the top side just over the filling and seal with water.

**5.**

Pull the 'bottom lip' up over the 'top lip' of the dough. Pinch firmly to seal the juicy filling inside.

**6.**

⚠ This is easiest when done with a second pair of hands. Place the filled dough, seam side down, onto a lightly greased baking sheet. Shape into one side of a heart.

**7.**

Repeat with the second half of the dough and cherries. Remember to seal tightly. Place the second half onto the baking sheet across from the first, completing the heart. Pinch well to connect the two sides.

**8.** Cover and let rise until double in size, about one hour. Preheat oven to 350°.

**9.** ⚠ Bake until golden brown, about 25 to 30 minutes. Carefully remove heart from baking sheet to the cooling rack.

**10.**

When the heart has cooled, ice with white frosting and shake on Valentine sprinkles.

**TOOLS:** 6-cup capacity oven-proof bowl, baking sheet, non-stick cooking spray, rolling pin, pizza cutter, ruler, small bowl of water, 12-inch by 12-inch square of aluminum foil, scissors

# MAY BASKETS

A special tradition on the first day of May is to fill a small basket with flowers or sweets, lay it on a friend's or neighbor's doorstep, ring the bell and RUN!

Bake at 375°
for 20
minutes
plus
6-8 minutes

**Things You'll Need:**

**2 Batches of White Dough**
(Page 30)

**You can color dough if you like.**

Quinsey made a simpler version. She coiled skinny ropes of dough around a greased ball of foil.

After it had baked and cooled, she removed the foil and filled her little basket with jelly beans as a May Day surprise.

Ready for a challenge? Our beautiful May Baskets proved to be the most difficult technique for our kids <u>and</u> adult helpers alike!

But fear not. Carefully read the instructions on Pages 102 and 103 all the way through.

Be prepared to have your first basket (or two) be an educational experience.

The good news is, once you master the technique, you will be able to produce May Baskets with ease.

The person who receives your basket will hold this creation and your baking skills in awe!

**1.**

Place bowl upside down on a greased baking sheet. Spray bowl and area around bowl with cooking spray.

**2.**

Place both batches of dough onto lightly floured work surface. Cut one fourth off of each ball and set aside for the basket's rim.

**3.**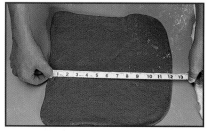

Roll the remaining dough pieces into two 12-inch by 12-inch squares.

**4.**

Make one inch marks on the top and bottom of the squares. Then use a pizza cutter to cut 12 strips from each square.

**5.**

Select the 8 best strips of each color. Carefully move 8 strips of the first color onto the aluminum foil.

**6.**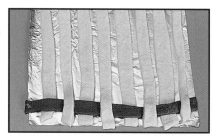

Using a strip of the 2nd color, weave "under-over-under-over" all the way across the mat of strips.·

**7.** Weave another strip of the second color "over-under-over-under" all the way across the mat. Keep the strips close together. Repeat weaving process with the 6 other strips of the second color. (You will have extra strips of both colors. A fun use for the extras is to cut and tie them into little knots, let rise and bake for dinner rolls.)

**8.**

Use pizza cutter to trim the strips even with the foil. Preheat oven to 375°.

**9.**

Roll the dough you set aside in Step 2 into two 24-inch ropes. Moisten at one end and pinch together. Twist ropes around each other. Seal opposite end with a dab of water.

**10.**

Lay twisted rope around the bowl's rim. Wet fingers and pinch ends together to complete the circle.

**11.**

⚠ Slide hands under foil and lift gently, turning over and placing woven dough so it rests on the bowl.

**12.**

Peel off aluminum foil and set aside.

**13.**

Use scissors to trim off strips where they touch the pan. Pull dough rim out slightly and tuck strips inside the rim.

**14.** ⚠ Bake for 20 minutes, then ⚠ place the aluminum foil square over basket to keep from burning. Bake another 6 to 8 minutes until rim is browned.

**15.** ⚠ Remove basket from bowl. Place on wire rack to cool, rim side down.

**TOOLS:** dough cutter, two baking sheets, plastic wrap, cooking spray, egg wash, pastry brush

# JULY 4TH BURGER BUNS

Bake at 375°
for 15-20
minutes

## DOUGH

### Baker's Choice

– **White** (Page 30)
– **Garlic** (Page 46)
– **Multigrain** (Page 62)

### Toppings:

• **Sesame seeds**
• **Toasted onion**
• **Poppy seeds**

**1.**

On lightly floured work surface, divide dough into 6 equal pieces.

**2.**

Gently roll each piece into a nice round ball.

**3.**

Place on lightly greased baking sheet. Gently shape. Buns should be round and about 1-inch thick.

**4.**

Lightly spray buns with cooking spray and cover buns with plastic wrap. Lay another baking sheet on top to help shape the buns.

**5.**

After 30 minutes, remove the top baking sheet and the plastic wrap. Preheat oven to 375°. Brush the buns with egg wash.

**6.**

Sprinkle the buns with the toppings you like.

**7.** ⚠ Bake until golden brown, about 15 to 20 minutes. Cool on wire rack before ⚠ slicing in half.

**Fun With Buns:**

• For a festive touch at your holiday barbecue, let your family and friends pick from red, white or blue buns. Make three batches of dough; color one red and another blue.

• Making dough that matches the colors of your sports team's jerseys is a huge hit at team parties.

• If you want to make hot dog buns, divide the dough ball into eight, and form each piece into the size and shape of a hot dog.

**TOOLS:** dough cutter, rolling pin, egg wash, pastry brush, extra large baking sheet

# THE WITCH HEAD

## WHAT YOU'LL NEED:

- 1 batch of plain White Bread dough (Page 30)
- 1 batch of White Bread dough colored green (Pages 26 & 30)
- Bottle of poppy seeds
- 1 black olive
- 1 green olive
- 3 Hot Tamales®
  (cinnamon flavored candies)

Bake at 350°
for 20-25
minutes

**1.**  On lightly floured surface, form the white dough into a log. Cut in half. Cut one of these pieces in half.

**2.**  Roll one of the small pieces into a triangle for the hat. Stretch the base with your hands as needed.

**3.**  Roll the other small piece into a rectangle and set it aside to make the brim of the hat later.

**4.**  Hold the large piece of dough firmly and yank the bottom out to make the chin.

**5.**  Grab the middle of the dough and pull out a long nose.

**6.**  Lay the hat triangle onto lightly greased baking sheet, with the tip in the upper left hand corner. Lay the face just beneath the hat. Press in the green olive for the eye and the black olive wart on the chin.

**7.**  Roll a small short rope of green dough for an eyebrow. Place above the "eye" and press lightly.

**8.**  Cut the green dough into 5 pieces. Then make each piece into a braid for hair. (Page 74)

**9.**  Arrange the "hair" on the pan for that "wind blown" look. Add bangs using a small piece of one braid.

**10.**  Re-roll the "brim" rectangle. Carefully stretch and place where the hat meets the face. Preheat oven to 350°.

**11.** Egg wash the hat and brim. Cover with poppy seeds. Be careful not to sprinkle seeds on the face.

**12.**  Use your finger to make a "lip groove" for the red Hot Tamales to be placed into after baking.

**13.** ⚠ Bake for 20 to 25 minutes watching closely so your witch's hair doesn't get too brown!

**14.**  ⚠ Remove to wire rack. When cool, insert red candy lips.

# Halloween Party Tips...

- Use a batch of orange colored dough to make soup bowls that look like little pumpkins. (Page 76)
- ⚠ To turn a punch bowl into a bubbling cauldron of "witch's brew," have a grown-up add dry ice to your favorite party drink. While chilling the punch, the dry ice will also make it bubble and steam!

**TOOLS:** rolling pin, pizza cutter, scissors, baking sheet, small bowl of water

# FALL HARVEST BREADSTICKS

Grown-ups might not believe how easy it was for you to make this stunning Thanksgiving masterpiece — and you may not want to tell them, either!

Bake at 350° for 20-25 minutes

## JoJo says...

"My family thought this was too beautiful to eat, but they changed their mind when I pulled a piece off for them to try!"

• If you brush this lightly with butter when it comes out of the oven, the crust will be soft and shiny.

• If your grocery store doesn't sell cracked wheat, try your local health food store.

## DOUGH RECIPE

**Water**
1 cup

**White Bread Flour**
2 cups

**Wheat Bread Flour**
1 cup

**Dry Milk**
2 Tablespoons

**Sugar**
1/4 cup

**Salt**
2 teaspoons

**Butter**
3 Tablespoons

**Honey**
2 Tablespoons

**Cracked Wheat**
2 Tablespoons

**Bran Flakes**
1 Tablespoon

**Oat Bran**
1 Tablespoon

**Yeast**
fast rise
1 + 1/2 teaspoons
**-or-**
**Yeast**
active dry
2 teaspoons

**1.** Set aside one-quarter of the dough for making stems.

**2.** Roll the large dough piece into a 9-inch by 18-inch rectangle.

**3.** Cut into 18 short strips. Set two strips aside for the bow.

**4.** Using a downward slant, snip almost to the middle every 1/4-inch down one side of the strip.

**9.** Let rise for 30 minutes. Preheat oven to 350°. ⚠ Bake until golden brown, about 20 to 25 minutes.

**5.** Turn the strip over and snip the other side, using the same downward slant. When snipped on both sides, it should look like a series of arrows. Complete remaining dough strips.

**6.** Layer the strips onto the top portion of a lightly greased baking sheet so the arrows point down. They should look like a bouquet of wheat stalks.

**7.** Roll all of the remaining dough into 4-inch ropes the thickness of a crayon. Layer the ropes as stems below the snipped stalks.

**8.** Using the two reserved strips, make a bow as shown on Page 139. Place the bow where the stems and stalks meet, attaching with a dab of water.

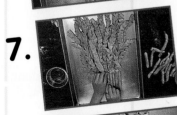

**TOOLS:** dough cutter, 2 baking sheets, paper towel, 2 bowls or pans

# CHRISTMAS TREE

Bake at 325° for 25-30 minutes

## DOUGH RECIPE

**Water**
1 cup

**White Bread Flour**
3 cups

**Dry Milk**
2 Tablespoons

**Sugar**
3 Tablespoons

**Salt**
1 teaspoon

**Butter**
3 Tablespoons

**Yeast**
fast rise
1 teaspoon
**-or-**
**Yeast**
active dry
1 + 1/2 teaspoons

# Amy says...

"It's messy, it's fun and it's beautiful when it's done!"

While you're in the holiday mood, see the Christmas Tree technique in the Bread as Art section (Page 136). For more holiday fun, try making Christmas candy canes using the Valentine's heart technique (Page 98).

**1.**
Put 16 maraschino cherries, without stems, onto paper towels to drain.

**2.**
Divide dough into 16 equal pieces on lightly floured work surface.

**3.**
Pat one piece to flatten slightly.

**4.**
Press a drained cherry into the center of the piece.

**5.**
Use the "Pouch Pinch" (Page 25) technique to hide the cherry inside.

**6.**
Gently roll back and forth between your palms to make a smooth round ball. Repeat with other pieces.

**7.**
Roll all 16 balls in the beaten egg and set aside on a baking sheet. Wash and dry your hands.

**8.**
Roll the largest ball in the chocolate sprinkles. Place at the bottom of lightly greased baking sheet for the tree's trunk.

**9.**
Roll the other 15 balls in the green sugar, coating completely.

**10.**
Lay balls in rows as shown to make the tree. The bottom row should have 5 balls.

**11.** Let rise until almost double in size, about 1 hour. Preheat oven to 325°.

**12.** ⚠ Bake, about 25 to 30 minutes. ⚠ When done remove from oven, cool 5 minutes and carefully remove to serving platter.

**TOOLS:** dough cutter, resealable plastic bag, paper towels, 2 bowls or pie pans, 2 baking sheets, aluminum foil

# HOLIDAY WREATH

Bake at 325° for 20 minutes plus 10-15 minutes

## What You'll Need:

**1 batch of dough**
(Page 110)

**Green Food Coloring**
4-5 drops

**Coconut**
3 cups

**Maraschino Cherries**
2 8-ounce jars, drained

**1 Egg**
beaten

**1.** Remove stems and put cherries on paper towels to drain. (See Step 1, Page 111.)

**2.** Color coconut green by shaking in a sealed plastic bag with 4 to 5 drops of green liquid food coloring.

**3.**

On lightly floured work surface, form a dough log. Cut off a 1/3 piece.

**4.**

Divide largest piece of dough into 16 pieces. Then make 15 pieces out of the smaller section.

**5.**

Use the "Pinch Pouch" technique (Page 25) to hide a cherry in the center of each piece of dough.

**6.**

Roll each cherry-filled piece of dough in beaten egg and set aside on a baking sheet. Remember to wash your hands after this step

**7.**

Next roll each ball in the green coconut. Be sure to have a thick layer of coconut, covering the ball completely.

**8.** Place the 15 smaller balls in a circle on a lightly greased baking sheet. Then place the 16 large balls around the outer edge of the first circle.

**9.**

Decorate your wreath by placing remaining cherries between the two circles as shown.

**10.** Let rise until double in size or about 1 hour. Preheat oven to 325°.

**11.** ⚠ Cook at 325° for 20 minutes. Then cover wreath with aluminum foil and bake for approximately 10 to 15 minutes more. Watch closely to avoid over-browning the coconut.

# LET'S PARTY!

**TOOLS:** dough or pizza cutter, rolling pin, scissors, small strainer, two baking sheets

# SNOWFLAKE PARTY

## The perfect theme for Snow Boarding, Sledding, Skating or Skiing!

Bake at 375° for 10-12 minutes

## Invitations

Use the same folding and cutting technique with paper to make "snowflake" invitations for your party.

### DOUGH RECIPE

**Water**
1 cup

**White Bread Flour**
3 cups

**Dry Milk**
2 Tablespoons

**Sugar**
3 Tablespoons

**Salt**
1 teaspoon

**Butter**
3 Tablespoons

**Yeast**
fast rise
1 teaspoon
-or-
**Yeast**
active dry
1 + 1/2 teaspoons

## Emily says.....

"It's really fun for my friends if the dough is ready when they get to my house. Everyone makes snowflakes and then my Mom bakes them while my Dad takes us sledding. We eat them with hot cocoa or spiced cider to warm us up when we get home!"

**See Party Kit on Page 167**

116

**1.**

Preheat oven to 375°. On lightly floured workspace, divide dough into 8 equal pieces.

**2.**

Roll each piece into a 6-inch square or circle.

**3.**

Lightly re-flour workspace. Flip each piece to flour both sides. Fold in half, but do NOT press together. Re-flour and fold your dough over a second time.

**4.**

Make scissor cuts along the outside edges, snipping left and right to cut small pieces out.

**5.**

Lay the snowflake onto lightly greased baking sheet and gently unfold it.

**6.** ⚠ Bake until golden brown, about 10 to 12 minutes, and remove to wire racks. Brush warm snowflakes with melted butter.

**7.**

When cool, sprinkle snowflakes lightly with powdered sugar.

**TOOLS:** baking sheets, cooking spray, six 4-inch metal baking rings, dough cutter, heavy-duty aluminum foil, pizza cutter or scissors, small bowl of water

# SUPER SLEUTH PARTY

**Bake at 375°
12 minutes,
plus 8-10 minutes**

Here's the perfect party for friends who like to unravel mysteries.

## What You'll Need:
- **Sweet Dough** (Page 32)
- **Jolly Ranchers® Hard Candy**
- **Egg Wash**
- **Sprinkles**

## Invitations:

Write invitations in code by assigning a number to each letter of the alphabet. Include a key to your code on the back, so everyone can solve the first mystery — and get to your party!

The fun begins with each detective making his/her own magnifying glass. Each guest selects the Jolly Rancher® flavors of choice and leaves them with the kitchen crew for the final baking steps. The guests then set off on a treasure hunt. Clues (written as riddles or rhymes) lead your friends from one hiding place to the next. A small treat and the next clue can be revealed at each stop. Or each clue might lead to another clue, with all of the treasure at the final stop. Guests return to enjoy their freshly baked, beautiful magnifying glasses!

**1.**

Cover 2 baking sheets with aluminum foil and spray with non-stick cooking spray. On lightly floured work surface, cut dough into 6 equal pieces.

**2.**

Roll each piece into a 20-inch rope using the "gravity" technique (Page 75, step 2). Roll rope back and forth gently on the work surface to get a smooth rope.

**3.**

Wrap one rope around a greased metal ring until the circle is complete and the dough overlaps slightly. Dab a little water where the dough layers meet and pinch to seal.

**4.**

Lay the handle straight down from the circle. Use a pizza cutter or scissors to cut handle into three strips. Braid strips tightly and seal ends.

**5.**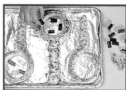

With one hand, slide your fingers into the circle, holding dough and ring together. Use other hand to lift the handle as you move the magnifying glass onto the greased, foiled baking sheet. Complete remaining ropes placing three glasses onto each baking sheet.

**6.**

Egg wash and add sprinkles. Cover and let rise 30 minutes. Preheat oven to 375°.

The steps to make these are tricky – but the results are amazing!

**7.** ⚠ Bake for 12 minutes. Remove from oven.

**8.**

⚠ Carefully remove baking rings.

**9.**

⚠ Drop 5 unwrapped Jolly Ranchers® into each circle. Put pan back into oven and bake 8 to 10 more minutes, until candy is melted and bubbly, but not brown.

**10.**

⚠ Remove from oven. Carefully slide aluminum foil sheets from pans onto cooling racks. (A bath towel will work if you don't have large enough racks.)

**11.** Let cool 10 minutes. ⚠ Then peel foil off. If foil sticks, let glasses cool another minute or two.

**12.** Carefully turn candy-side up to finish cooling. Eat the same day or freeze.

**See Party Kit on Page 167**

**I**nvitations: Blow up a balloon, but don't tie it. Use thin-line permanent markers to write your invitation on the balloon. Let the air out and mail the invite to your friend!

**Y**ou and your friends can create your own Backyard Circus! Ask every guest to bring a stuffed 'wild' animal so they can be a part of the show you'll put on for each other. Be ready with dress-up clothes and funny hats, and several hula hoops for your dog (or little sister) to jump through.

# CIRCUS PARTY

**F**eed the hungry crowds with your favorite sandwich fillings between slices of colored braids (Page 74).

**See Party Kit on Page 167**

**G**ive everyone a snack-sized plastic bag of pennies when they arrive, so they can 'buy' balloons with curling ribbon strings, paper bags of popcorn and chances to play the games.

**F**reeze purple or red 100% fruit juice into ice cubes for your pink lemonade. Unless you have your own cotton candy machine, multi-colored Popsicles® make a great dessert!

**A** few carnival booths (like bean bag toss or water balloon bowling) would round out the fun.

Ask a talented volunteer to paint faces (or feet or knees or cheeks!)

**TOOLS:** dough cutter, baking sheet, small bowl of water, egg wash, pastry brush

# BUNNY BRUNCH

Bake at 350°
for 18-22
minutes

**DOUGH**

## Baker's Choice

– **Sweet** (Page 32)
– **Ginger** (Page 34)
– **Chocolate** (Page 36)

Serve a bunny brunch at your next slumber party. Before you settle in for a night of videos, spend some time in the kitchen. Turn a batch of bread dough into six adorable bunnies! Then cover the bunnies with plastic wrap, refrigerate and bake using steps 5, 6, and 7 on Page 97. Enjoy a bunny brunch late the next morning.

If you're having the brunch at Easter, make your egg hunt fun for all ages. Buy plastic eggs in a variety of colors. Choose one color for each guest, so the level of trickiness can be matched to the age of the "seeker." Everyone should have the same number of eggs to look for, with the same surprises inside, so the fun will be in the challenge of the hunt!

For a more formal brunch, make the bunnies ahead of time and write each guest's name across the bunny's tummy with decorator icing. Use the bunnies as place cards at the table to show each guest where to sit.

**1.**

On lightly floured work surface, divide the dough into 6 equal pieces.

**2.**

Shape each piece of dough into a log. Each log will become one bunny.

**3.**

Cut the first log in half. Set aside one piece for the bunny's body. Cut the other piece in half and divide one of these halves into four equal pieces for the bunny's legs. Cut the remaining piece in half to be used for the bunny's head and ears.

**4.**

Use the largest dough piece to form an oval body and place on the baking sheet. Then form the head from the next largest piece. Attach the head to the body by pinching a tab at the neck, dabbing it with water and placing it under the body.

**5.**

Carefully pull a tiny bit of dough from the body for the nose. Roll into a ball and attach with a dab of water. Make balls out of the four smallest pieces and attach as legs by pinching a tab, dabbing with water, and placing under the body.

**6.**

Cut the remaining dough piece in half and roll into ropes for the ears.

**7.**

Form a skinny "U" with each rope and place the ends under the bunny's head to form the ear. Have fun giving your bunnies lopsided ears like bunnies in real life.

**8.**

Create five more bunnies with the remaining dough logs using the above steps.

**9.** Cover and let rise until double in size, about 1 hour. Preheat oven to 350°. Brush tops of bunnies lightly with egg wash.

**10.** ⚠ Bake until golden brown, about 18 to 22 minutes. Remove to cooling rack.

123

**TOOLS:** dough cutter, small bowl of water, scissors, baking sheet

# SPACE PARTY

Bake at 350° for 18-22 minutes

**What You'll Need:**
A variety of colored doughs
(Page 26 - 27)

The universe is an exciting place — every alien you make will have its own special look! Making aliens is a double kind of fun...you get one great look before they're baked and a different, eerie appearance after they're done.

Creating Space Alien Heads is the main activity of this party! Our kids in the kitchen enjoyed rolling, pinching and snipping, making a whole galaxy of creatures. You and your friends will come up with your own variations like our kids did — including using more than one color inside and 'tie-dye' doughs.

The bravest among you may decide to use the "Pouch Pinch" (Page 25) technique to hide chocolate chips, a caramel or a cube of your favorite cheese in the inside dough ball, to make each alien bite a warm, oozy treat.

Decorate the walls and ceiling of your dining room with glow-in- the-dark stars. Then turn off the lights when it's time to eat. Out of this world!

Before baking    After baking

**1.**

Select and cut a piece of colored dough for the inside color of the head. (Ping pong to baseball size!)

**2.**

Form the dough into a ball.

**3.** Cut a piece of different colored dough for the outside of the alien's head, about the same size as the inside ball.

**4.**

Pat or roll into a disc large enough to cover the inside ball.

**5.**

Use the "Pouch Pinch" technique to completely hide the inside ball of dough (Page 25). Dab with water and pinch tightly to seal. Roll gently in palms to make a smooth ball.

**6.**

Turn the head over and scissor-snip as many features as you choose: eyes, nose, mouth, ears, hair... Make deep snips so the inside color will show after rising. Antennae, hair or tongues can also be added by layering (Page 136).

**7.**

Place on a lightly greased baking sheet. Cover and let rise until double in size, about 1 hour. Preheat oven to 350°.

**8.** ⚠️Bake for about 18 to 22 minutes, cool slightly, and be brave enough to bite!

**We Come In Peace ...** Want to go to Mars? Study hard, and learn to use your bread machine. At the Johnson Space Center in Texas, NASA has been learning what it takes to survive on Mars by having people live inside a three-level life support chamber for months at a time. The test crew members recycle air and water, grow fresh lettuce, and do their baking in a bread machine. NASA's chief scientist thinks a mission to Mars may be possible by 2013 or sooner.

**See Party Kit on Page 167**

**TOOLS:** dough cutter, small bowl of water, scissors, extra large baking sheet

# BOOK LOVERS' BASH

Bake at 350° for 30-35 minutes

If the weather is too blustery for outdoor fun, phone your friends and invite them over! Have everyone come dressed as a character from one of their favorite books. Play 20 Questions (the answers always have to be Yes or No) to discover who each person is pretending to be.

A Tag-Along story could come next, with the guests sitting in a circle. One person starts the chain by briefly telling the beginning of their character's story. The next person picks up with a part of their book's story, building a wacky new tale as each guest adds in a portion from their favorite book.

Dip raw veggies, breadsticks and your favorite chips into the Snowman's bowl for extra energy while you play!

**TIP:** Make an extra batch of dough and divide it among your buddies when they arrive. Let everyone make their own mini-snowman. Use mini-chocolate chips for the face, raisins for buttons and pretzel sticks for the arms. Serve them warm at the end of the party or send home as a reminder of your great afternoon.

**1.**
On lightly floured surface, shape each batch of dough into a log.

**2.**
Cut the two logs into five pieces, as shown.

**3.**
Form the two largest pieces into smooth, round balls for the Snowman's base and belly.

**4.**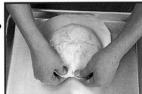
Place the base at the bottom edge of the lightly greased baking sheet. Place the belly <u>upside</u> down on top of the base. Dab edges with water and pinch to attach. Then carefully unfold onto the baking sheet.

**5.**
Use the smallest dough piece to roll a rope for the scarf and curve around the top of the belly. Fringe the end of the scarf with scissors. Moisten to seal between scarf and belly.

**6.**
Create the Snowman's head with the largest remaining dough piece. Dab with water and attach to scarf.

**7.**
Cut 1-inch strip off the last dough piece. Flatten the rest into a hat.

**8.**
Snip the strip in half. Roll one half of strip into a brim for the hat.

**9.**
Place hat and brim onto the pan. Dab with water and pinch to attach.

**10.**
Form two eyes and a smile out of the last bit of dough. Attach them by dabbing with water and pressing gently.

**11.** Cover and let rise until double in size, about one hour. Preheat oven to 350°. ⚠ Bake until golden brown, about 30 to 35 minutes.

**12.** ⚠Remove to wire rack. When cool use Soup Bowl technique (Page 76) to form dip bowl in Snowman's base.

127

**TOOLS:** dough cutter, rolling pin or dough roller, baking sheets, corn meal, pizza cutter

# PIZZA PARTY

Bake at 400° for 12-20 minutes

## Toppings:
- Bottle of pizza sauce
- 2 cups mozzarella cheese

### Baker's Choice
- Pepperoni • Ham
- Mushrooms • Pineapple
- Olives • Green pepper
- Onions

Pizza Parties are great afternoon or evening fun for kids of all ages. Send out construction paper invitations that look like pizza or get several small pizza boxes from a local pizza place, put invitations inside and deliver dressed like a pizza delivery person.

## DOUGH RECIPE

**Water**
1 + 1/2 cups

**White Bread Flour**
4 cups

**Sugar**
2 Tablespoons

**Salt**
2 teaspoons

**Yeast**
fast rise
2 teaspoons
-or-
**Yeast**
active dry
3 teaspoons

The day of the party turn your kitchen into your very own pizzeria by setting out tools, batches of dough, squeeze bottle sauce, and lots of bowls of assorted toppings. When your friends arrive they'll head straight to the kitchen and "build" their way to dinner. While pizzas are baking our younger kids enjoyed a "pin the pepperoni on the pizza" game. Our teenagers, on the other hand, preferred a scavenger hunt.

• Our technique shows six individual pizzas. However, you might choose to make one large pizza, or four deep dish pizzas with the personal pizza pans shown on Page 166.

**1.**

Preheat oven to 400°. Divide dough into 6 equal pieces.

**2.**

Each pizza maker gets their own piece of dough to round gently into a ball.

**3.**

Roll dough to the size and thickness you want. Dough 1/4-inch thick produces a regular crust. Thick dough will give a chewy crust and thin will make it crispy.

**4.**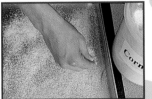

Lightly grease baking sheets and sprinkle well with cornmeal.

**5.**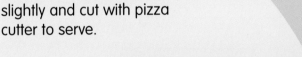

Place pizza onto baking sheets. Spread sauce on dough and add cheese.

**6.**

Add other toppings you like.

**7.** ⚠ Bake for 12 to 20 minutes, until crust is golden brown and cheese is bubbly. Let cool slightly and cut with pizza cutter to serve.

**See Party Kit on Page 167**

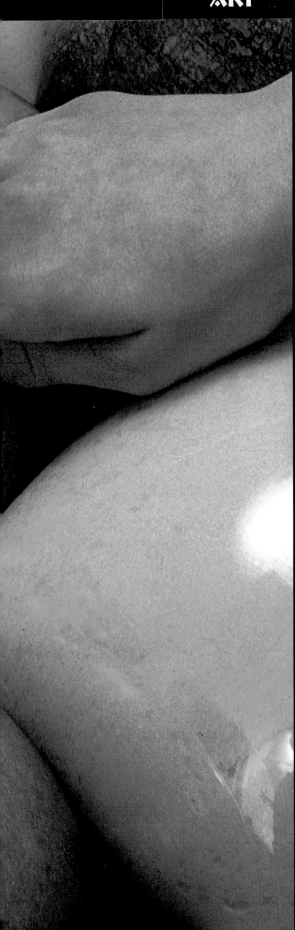

# BREAD
# AS ART

# BREAD AS ART

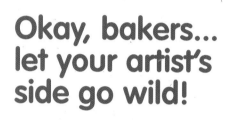

Serpent by Kati, age 13

## Okay, bakers... let your artist's side go wild!

Join our kids in the fun of using bread dough to create beautiful art that's tasty, too!

## Basic Tips...

Unlike Playdough® that stays where you put it, the yeast makes bread dough lively. It's springy and will contract a little each time you form it.

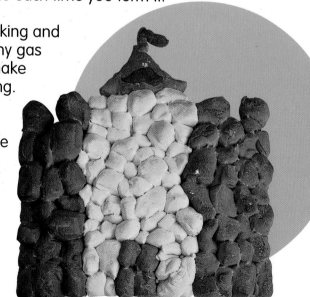

**Octopus by Ashley, age 11**

Be gentle. Whacking and smacking and twirling will pop the tiny gas bubbles hidden in your bread that make your bread light and tasty after baking.

Keep the thickness of your dough pieces about the same for your whole project, unless you want a part to balloon up like Ashley's octopus.

Galen built his castle (right) onto a greased baking sheet. It was a tasty treat fit for a king!

**Castle by Galen, age 8**

# Making a rainbow of colors...

Make several batches of White Bread dough, (Page 30) adding paste food coloring to the water. Or make one recipe of White dough and divide the dough into quarters. Use your bread machine to color each piece, being careful to completely clean and dry your bread machine pan between each color. (See coloring doughs on Page 26.)

**Violets by Kelsey, age 12**

Store each color of dough in an air-tight bag. Dough can be stored in your refrigerator or freezer (Page 27).

**Fish by Marisa, age 11**

For an art party, invite friends who have bread machines to each make a color or two and bring dough to your house for a baking adventure.

# Creating your art shape...

There are two basic ways to build dough art.

**1.** Form dough into balls, ropes and other shapes then join by layering or pinching together firmly with wet fingers.

**Doll by Molly, age 10**

**2.** Roll dough out on lightly floured work surface and cut the shape out with scissors or a ⚠ small knife. It's helpful to "draw" the outline lightly with the knife tip before you cut or use a paper pattern. Andrew created this two-headed dragon using the cut-out technique.

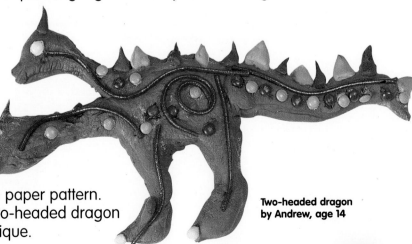

**Two-headed dragon by Andrew, age 14**

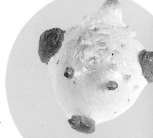

# Creature Creations...

It's fun to make creatures, real and imaginary, using brightly colored dough and some creative dough techniques.

Cale created this hedgehog from a football-shaped piece of dough. He used scissors to create the furry texture for the body. After baking, he added green candy eyes.

**Hedgehog by Cale, age 10**

**Blowfish by Megan, age 13**

# Snipping details...

Use scissors as a decorating tool — simply snip the dough to create scales, spikes and tentacles. Make deep cuts with the scissors so the cuts don't close up during rising and baking. Change the angle of the cuts to achieve the look you want.

# Cutting blocks...

You can make building blocks (or bricks) by rolling out a rectangle of thick dough and then cutting rows of "bricks" to build a castle (like the one on Page 132), or any other dwelling. You can also use scissors to cut strips or thick ropes of dough into cubes.

**Crocodile by Molly, age 10**

Martin covered an oven-proof bowl with greased aluminum foil to use as the base for the igloo he built out of dough cubes. The sugar snow was sprinkled on after it cooled.

**Igloo by Martin, age 10**
**Sugar snow by Ann, age 51**

# Creating ropes & spirals...

Perhaps one of the simplest techniques to make fun shapes is rolling the dough into ropes and coiling them to form snails, flowers and beehives.

Make ropes by rolling a small piece of dough on the work surface with the palms of your hands.

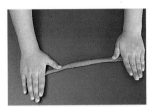

To make a spiral (as for the snail or beehive pictured on this page), make a long slender rope and curl one end. Continue wrapping the rope in circles.

**Snail by Rosey, age 6**

## Adding details...

To add details to your creation, like eyes, wings, legs, antennae and leaves, attach them by wetting fingers, dabbing dough and pinching firmly. Use toothpicks as supports to keep little details in while baking.

**Bee by Joanna, age 9**

**Rose by Kelsey, age 12**

**Beehive by James, age 9**

# Layering...

Building one level of dough on top of another is called "layering." One way to achieve great results is to combine the layering technique with the cut-out technique. To add a layer, wet the dough with water and attach a new layer on top. Gently press the dough together so it sticks.

Kyle created the King of Hearts card and a Mountain Sunrise using a combination of the layering technique and the cutout technique. For his sunrise he cut out the mountains and then he layered on snowy peaks. When designing the card, he cut out a rectangle shape, then added another layer of dough on top to create the king and the hearts. It's royal!

**King of Hearts by Kyle, age 12**

**MountainSunrise by Kyle, age 12**

# Cutouts...

Create interesting art pieces by cutting shapes out of the dough. Called "cutouts," this technique is easy to do. Roll the dough out on a lightly floured work surface and cut out the shape with scissors or ⚠ small knife.

Sometimes it's helpful to "draw" the outline lightly with the tip of the knife before you cut out the design. Or use a paper pattern. Cut around the pattern then remove the excess dough (use it for another work of art).

**Tree by James, age 9 & Andy, age 13**

# Adding decorations...

Decorate your art with bits of dough or use candies (like m&m's® and baking chips) that don't melt in the oven. Press candy firmly into dough. **Do not** use water to attach the candy. Water could cause the candy to melt and lose its shape.

Bug by Andy, age 13

Clown by Marisa, age 11

Katie and Nyaling had lots of fun creating this elf. They worked together to get just the right look. The elf was made using many of the techniques described in this chapter. The body, head and hat were all formed from dough balls. The face was made of small bits of dough attached with water. The decorations for the elf's outfit are colored sprinkles. The silver balls at the tips of his boots are baker's decorations. From the smile on his face, it looks like this elf found his pot of gold!

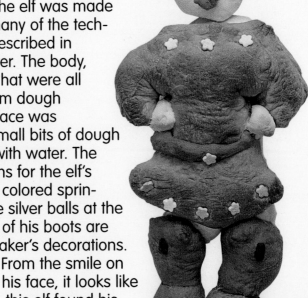

Elf by Kati, age 13
Boots by Nyaling, age 8

Robot Caterpillar by Alexandra, age 4

Crab by Andy, age 13

# Puffy creations...

As you work, keep in mind that dough rises and your creation will grow. For thick dough creations like the crab, Andy waited until after the dough had risen to add the features. Otherwise the decorations may have popped off the crab as the dough rose.

Pig by Rosey, age 6

Rosey used the puffiness of the dough to make the belly of her pig balloon up.

The airplane and car shown here are examples of what can happen if small details are added before the dough has risen. Note the windows of the plane were blown off the body and landed on the wings during baking.

Airplane by Andy, age 13

This car just puffed up all over. So it became a hot-air flying machine after baking. That's called creative license!

Flying machine by James, age 9

# Combining techniques...

The mermaid was made by rolling the dough and cutting it to form the shape of the body and the fish tail. Ropes of dough were added to make her hair. Layering was used to add her facial features and clothing. Then the snipping technique was used to make her scales.

**Mermaid by Kati, age 13**

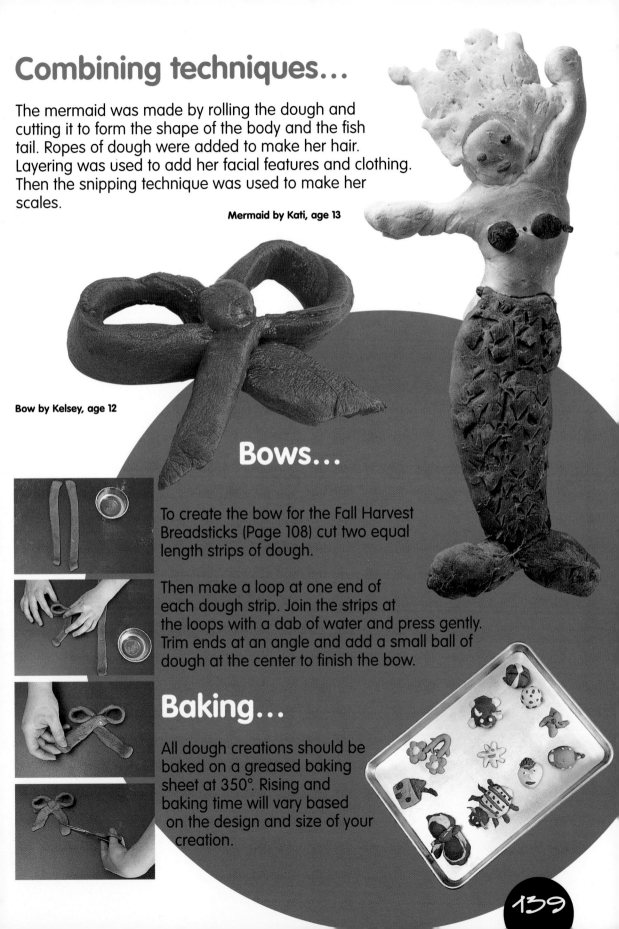

**Bow by Kelsey, age 12**

## Bows...

To create the bow for the Fall Harvest Breadsticks (Page 108) cut two equal length strips of dough.

Then make a loop at one end of each dough strip. Join the strips at the loops with a dab of water and press gently. Trim ends at an angle and add a small ball of dough at the center to finish the bow.

## Baking...

All dough creations should be baked on a greased baking sheet at 350°. Rising and baking time will vary based on the design and size of your creation.

# ELECTRIC BREAD GOES TO SCHOOL

# A DAY AT SCHOOL

**Good Morning, Class ... We're going to have fun today. We'll spend extra time getting ready for the Science Fair, as well as next Tuesday's bake sale.**

## MATH

**Flubber Buns: The Story Problem...** Cameron's soccer team, the "Flubbers," is having a cook-out to celebrate the end of their undefeated season. Cameron has been asked to bring three dozen hamburger buns, using the recipe from Page 104 of ***Electric Bread for Kids***. Each recipe makes six hamburger buns. You need to figure out how much of each ingredient he'll need (Hint: First figure out how many batches of the recipe you'll need to make.)

**Tasty Grams...** The tables on the next page will help you learn about metric measurement, and make your math exercises more fun. The recipes in this book were all tested in the ICE test kitchen using U.S. measurements and not metric equivalents. However, a skilled mathematician with a highly sensitive scale could convert the recipes to metric. Just for fun, pick your favorite recipe and use the conversion information to change the U.S measurements to metric. Invite your family to taste-test your math skills.

**Metric Conversions...** To figure out metric conversions, you either multiply by the U.S. unit, or divide by the metric unit. Either way you go, you use the same number. So, for example, to convert inches to centimeters, you would multiply by 2.54, and to convert centimeters to inches, you would divide by 2.54. A 12 inch pizza is 30.48 centimeters (cm) (12 x 2.54), and a 40 cm pizza is 15.75 inches across (40 ÷ 2.54). Got it? Exercise your brain or your calculator; hopefully, your recipe measurements will come out the same.

**Bake Sale Time...** On Tuesday, we're going to do a "delayed bake" with all of you bringing your bread machines from home. Bread will come out at 3:10 p.m., 10 minutes before our class bake sale starts. We'll have the best possible advertising — the aroma of Chocolate, Raisin and other delicious breads up and down the halls — and you'll have warm bread to slice for the sale. We will start all the bread machines at 9:00 a.m. Tuesday morning. Do the math to figure how to set your machine's timer and practice setting your machine at home.

# Metric Conversions

## Oven Temperature Equivalents

| Fahrenheit Setting | Celsius Setting |
|:---:|:---:|
| 300° | 150° |
| 325° | 160° |
| 350° | 175° |
| 375° | 190° |
| 400° | 200° |

## Approximate Measuring Equivalents

| U.S. Units | Metric | Inches | Centimeters |
|:---:|:---:|:---:|:---:|
| 1/4 teaspoon | 1.2 milliliter | 1 inches | 2.5 centimeters |
| 1/2 teaspoon | 2.5 milliliter | 8 inches | 20.3 centimeters |
| 1 teaspoon | 5 milliliter | 12 inches | 30.5 centimeters |
| 1 Tablespoon | 15 milliliter | 18 inches | 45.7 centimeters |
| 1/4 cup | 60 milliliter | 22 inches | 55.9 centimeters |
| 1/3 cup | 80 milliliter | | |
| 1/2 cup | 120 milliliter | | |
| 2/3 cup | 160 milliliter | | |
| 3/4 cup | 180 milliliter | | |
| 1 cup | 240 milliliter | | |
| 2 cups | 475 milliliter | | |
| 3 cups | 710 milliliter | | |
| 4 cups | 1 liter | | |

## Conversion Formulas

- teaspoons to milliliters, multiply the teaspoons by 4.93
- milliliters (ml) to teaspoons, divide the milliliters by 4.93

- Tablespoons to milliliters, multiply the Tablespoons by 14.79
- milliliters (ml) to Tablespoons, divide the milliliters by 14.79

- fluid ounces to milliliters, multiply the fluid ounces by 29.57
- milliliters (ml) to fluid ounces, divide the milliliters by 29.57

- cups to milliliters, multiply the cups by 236.59
- milliliters (ml) to cups, divide the milliliters by 236.59

- inches to centimeters, multiply the inches by 2.54
- centimeters to inches, divide the centimeters by 2.54

143

# BREAD MACHINE BAKING DEMONSTRATION

**Today class, Martin will demonstrate how to make White Bread using a bread machine.**

**How The Bread Machine Works...** Some of us made bread in kindergarten. You combined all the ingredients in the big mixing bowl, let the bread rise, or "proof," punched it down and let it rise again, and then put it in the oven to bake. This is the same kind of bread, except the bread machine does everything for us once we put the ingredients into the bread pan.

With a bread machine, all you have to do is press a button on the machine's control unit and the machine's kneading blade mixes the ingredients and kneads the dough a first time. It lets the dough rest and kneads it again. Then it lets the dough rise and finally, it bakes the loaf. The heating element under your bread pan is hot, so an adult helper should take the pan out.

**Basic Ingredients for Bread...** Flour, yeast, water, sugar, salt and fat are the main ingredients in most breads. The dough is a mixture of these and other ingredients we choose to give our breads the flavor and texture we want. Let's talk about ingredients:

1 FLOUR
2 WATER
3 YEAST
4 SUGAR
5 DRY MILK
6 BUTTER
7 SALT

**Flour...** Flour is an important source of nutrients and it gives the bread its body. The best bread flour comes from wheat. You could make bread from just about any cereal grain, from rice to rye, but wheat gives the best results, mainly because it has the highest gluten content. When you add water it gets the gluten in gear. When we "work" the dough, which we call "kneading," it makes the gluten particles stronger and stickier. Once stuck together, the gluten keeps forming long continuous strands into an elastic mesh that traps the yeast's gas bubbles. Gluten is like muscles. The more you work them, the more developed they become. (If you don't work them at all, they'll be soft). But with bread gluten if you knead or work your dough too much, it can pro-duce a loaf that's flatter and tougher than you want. We're lucky, because the bread machine does all the work and knows how to make great gluten strands. For more about bread flour, see Page 160.

**Yeast...** It's alive!!! Yeast is not a plant, or an animal, but it is alive. It's a tiny one-celled fungus — so tiny that billions of cells go into each loaf of bread. Fungi can't produce their own food, so they feed on the things around them. Guess what? Yeast likes carbohydrates. It loves to feed on the natural sugar in grains. And for dessert, yeast loves any extra sugar, honey, molasses, or dried fruits we add to the bread.

When yeast is combined with moisture and warmth, it begins to "ferment," converting the flour's starch into alcohol and carbon dioxide gas. (The alcohol burns off in baking.) The gas forms little bubbles that try to head for the surface of the doughball, but ... they can't. They're trapped in the sticky web of gluten that holds them in the bread. This is what makes the bread rise, like a hot air balloon. When the bread rises, and is "punched down" again by the machine, it's bursting thousands of bubbles, making them smaller and more even in the dough. These gluten-trapped bubbles leave the little holes you see throughout your bread when you slice it.

**Water...** The liquid in your bread recipe brings your yeast to life, gets the gluten going, and is critical to a nicely textured loaf. Since water will activate the yeast, it's important to remember to keep the water separate from the yeast, especially on the "delayed bake" cycle.

**Sugar/Fruit...** Sugar not only adds flavor and helps brown the crust, but it feeds your yeast. There is sugar in raisins and other dried fruit. Add too much and you'll make the yeast go crazy, and the bread will rise too much.

**Salt...** Salt helps the flavor of your bread, but it also serves an important function: It puts the brakes on the fermenting, bubbling yeast and keeps it under control.

**Fat...** Fat makes your bread rich and moist, and helps make the texture soft. Most recipes use butter or margarine. Others use olive oil and other kinds of fat. Each gives its own flavor, but all do the same thing: Without the fat, your bread would be coarse, and wouldn't have as much flavor, or last as long. Too much fat will keep your bread from rising well because it works against the gluten. Remember those long gluten strands that form during kneading? Well, fat shortens the gluten strands. In fact, that's where the word "shortening" came from.

# DEMONSTRATION CHECKLIST

You can do a bread machine demonstration of your own. Use this page to prepare for taking your bread machine out to bake!

- ❏ Bread Machine

- ❏ Snacks — Make a loaf or two of bread before the demonstration and pack slices into a resealable plastic bag. Share during your demonstration.

- ❏ Bread Ingredients — Your demonstration will be easier if you premeasure ingredients into separate, resealable plastic bags. Label each bag with a permanent marker. Adjust this basic list below to include ingredients in the recipe you will be making.

**Dry Ingredients:**
- ❏ Flour
- ❏ Sugar
- ❏ Salt
- ❏ Dry Milk
- ❏ Other: _____
- ❏ Other: _____
- ❏ Other: _____
- ❏ Other: _____

**Refrigerated Items:**
- ❏ Yeast
- ❏ Butter
- ❏ Eggs
- ❏ Other: _____
- ❏ Other: _____

- ❏ *Electric Bread for Kids* — to show the class your recipe

- ❏ Liquid Measuring Cup — for measuring water

- ❏ Table Knife or Plastic Knife — for cutting butter cube

- ❏ Measuring Spoon — for measuring yeast, during demonstration

- ❏ Extension Cord — the electrical outlet may be far from your demonstration area

- ❏ Hot Pads — for removing bread from machine with an adult helper

- ❏ Bread Knife — for slicing bread with an adult helper

- ❏ Cutting Board — for slicing and serving bread

**ICE gives permission to anyone wishing to copy this checklist page
for classroom or family purposes. Enjoy!**

# HISTORY

**Here is Scott's report on the history of bread ...**

We call the process of turning grain into flour "milling," and for thousands of years people have been developing ways to make flour that gives us the best results. In ancient times, the wheat berries were crushed, which produced a coarse, bitter flour. In Egypt, where yeast breads have been made for over 4,000 years, one of the first tools to grind grain, rather than crushing it, was developed. It was called a "quern." For some time before the birth of Christ, water mills were used to grind grain into flour. Over a thousand years later, people began using windmills with sails. In both kinds of mills, two grinding stones were used. Modern millers use steel roller mills that allow them to grind flour to whatever fineness they like by adjusting the roller settings.

Buying bread at bakeries goes back to at least the Greek and Roman empires. In Italy in 79 A.D. a volcano flooded the town of Pompeii with lava. Archeologists digging through the preserved ruins of the city found breads in the village baking shops. Baking at home is now back in style. Big progress has been made in how we mix and bake our bread.

As the 20th century began, a small mechanical bread mixer won the Gold Medal at the 1904 World's Fair in St. Louis, Missouri. The 1908 Sears Catalogue offered a "Bread Mixer" for only $1.79. The catalogue said this was the best model on the market — "better than mixers offered by others at $4.00, $5.00 or even $6.00." With manual help, these machines mixed the dough and let it rise, similar to how we use a bread machine to make dough.

The bread machines we use today even bake the bread, something our great grandparents never imagined. These modern machines began making their way into American homes in the late 1980's. Soon, millions had been sold. Today, there are bread machines in over 20 million homes.

# LUNCH

Thanks to all 100 of you for joining us here in the cafeteria for our school's "Hunger Banquet." The $2 you each paid for your ticket is being sent to an organization that helps feed hungry children, like Oxfam America, which came up with the idea for this kind of banquet. Remember to write in your journal later how it felt to be part of this.

Now, the 15 of you who drew red tickets from the bowl by the door can be seated in a chair at the two middle tables with the fancy tablecloths and napkins, plates and silverware, and lighted candles. Enjoy your special turkey dinner, sparkling cider, and chocolate dessert. You represent the richest 15 percent of the world's population, the people who make over $8,900 a year, and are always able to eat well. Even though you're a small group, you consume 70 percent of the world's grains. You are healthier, go to better schools, and will live longer than those who drew blue or green tickets.

Next, will the 30 of you with the blue tickets take your places on the benches around these two tables. You'll get a bowl of soup and a carton of skim milk. You represent the 30 percent of the world's people who earn between $725 and $8,900 a year.

Okay, the rest of you – all 55 – please take your places on the floor once you have received your piece of bread and your cup of "dirty" (colored) water. You represent nearly 55 percent of the world's people. Almost a billion people live in awful poverty, making only $2 a day on average. Nearly 840 million experience hunger every day, 30 million of them in the United States.

Now, did I hear a little grumbling from some of you on the floor? Aren't you glad this is just one meal? Of course, it's not fair … but it's also not fair that one out of every four people in the world lives in poverty. It's unfair that every 2.5 seconds a child somewhere in the world dies from hunger or related causes — even though the world produces enough food to provide a decent meal to every man, woman and child.

Thank your lucky stars, most of us drew red tickets when we were born.

# SCIENCE

Science is lots of fun, in or out of school. Let's talk about how to do a science fair project, and then look at two ideas for experiments. You don't have to wait for your school's science fair — the kitchen is a great place to do a science experiment. Pick something that appeals to you. The object is always to have fun and learn something new.

**Plan Ahead...** Don't wait until the last minute to start your project. A good project requires that you spend time thinking about how it works, and some experiments are going to take time to do.

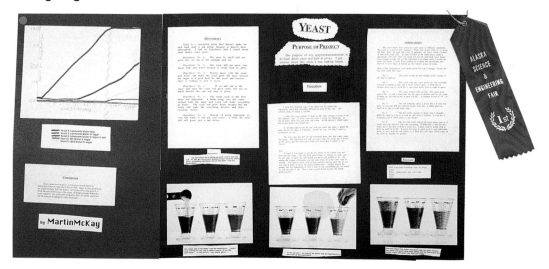

**A Method To Your Madness...** The experimental "scientific method" includes certain basic steps: Observation, Hypothesis, Controlled Experiment, and Conclusion. To actually perform a science experiment and exhibit it well, more steps may be needed.

Here are the basic steps:

• **Observe The World Around You....** It's the first step in any experiment. When you are curious about how or why something happens, you ask questions about it and check it out.

• **Identify What You Want To Study....** Make it specific and simple enough to have fun doing it. Don't pick something too general like, "learning all about fungi." There are over 100,000 species of fungi. Instead, look at something specific like, "What makes yeast grow?"

Scientists – http://atlas.ksc.nasa.gov/education/general/scifair.html • The Mad Scientist Network ("a collective crania of scientists answering questions in many areas") –

• **Research Your Subject....** Do your own work, but don't be afraid to consult other resources, including people — like real scientists do. Go to the library. Check the Internet. Keep track of your sources.

• **Identify Your Variables....** Things that can be changed are called variables. Change only one thing at a time in each experiment. (If you change more than one at a time, you won't know which variable is causing whatever you observe.)

• **Make A Hypothesis....** A hypothesis is a guess that can be tested by an experiment. Your guess or prediction is based on what you have learned in your investigation. Keep focused on a specific question and keep your experiment on track. As you learn more, your hypothesis can change.

• **Design Your Experiment....** Think out each step you will need to answer your guess. You should do at least one experiment to test each hypothesis. For an experiment to give answers you can trust, it must have a "control test" — exactly like the other tests, but without any variables changed.

• **Keep Records....** Keep track of what you do and observe, from the very start. Be precise in reporting the details of what you see. Record measurements made, amounts of things used, how long it took for things to happen, etc. Then, take time to summarize what happened. If you say, "the yeast mixture got a whole lot bigger after a while," instead of "after the first half hour, the yeast and sugar mixture doubled" you won't have a good basis for comparing results the next time you do it, and nobody else will be able to repeat your experiment.

• **Repeat Your Experiment....** Was it a fluke? If you can't reproduce your experiment you cannot trust your results.

• **Draw A Conclusion....** Analyze your results. Think about what you've found. Try to answer your original guesses. Is your hypothesis correct? If not, what could be the answer to your question? Summarize what you learned.

Don't worry if it turns out your hypothesis was wrong. Lots of important scientific discoveries are made by scientists who set out to prove one thing and find something different!

• **Write Your Report and Prepare Your Exhibit...** Present your work clearly and creatively.

# YEAST

**The Itsy Bitsy Fungi…** Molds and yeasts are microscopic organisms — we call them "organisms" because they are living things, and microscopic because each one is so tiny it can only be seen through a microscope. By the time colonies of yeast cells have grown enough that we can see them, there are billions of individual cells.

**They're Everywhere…** In addition to yeast sold in stores, there is yeast in the air all around us. There are lots of things you could do to experiment with yeast. How do different kinds work? You could study what would happen if you left a mixture of bread dough, without yeast, exposed to the air. Would it rise? (If it worked for the ancient Egyptians, it should work for you.) How much? How long would it take?

**Martin's Experiment…** Martin got interested in yeast after making bread for a while. He wanted to look at what kinds of things made yeast grow or kept it from growing. He knew from doing research that yeasts can't make their own food, that yeast feeds on the natural sugars in the starch from the wheat flour, and that other sugars make yeast grow even more.

**Getting Starting:** Adding yeast to beaker with water and sugar only.

**Control Test:** Mixing yeast with water only.

**Results:** Beaker with yeast/water/sugar grew more than yeast/water/sugar/salt and yeast/water only.

lass Hemiascomycetes. The true yeasts are found in one main order Saccharomycetales,

152

- **The More Things Change, The More They Stay The Same....** Martin wanted to see how a couple of different variables would affect the yeast, like the temperature of the water, the length of time it was left sitting, adding sugar, and adding salt. He wrote out his guesses about what would happen (his hypotheses) and designed his experiment so it would test each of these things. He used the same amount of water and yeast each time. He used one beaker with only lukewarm water and yeast each time as a "control."

**Been There, Done That....** You'll have fun trying your own yeast experiments. There are lots of possible ways to go about it. Here are a few tips Martin passes on:

- Martin found it was easier to pre-measure the dry things (yeast, sugar, etc.) and put them into the beakers first, before adding water. The dry stuff takes longer to measure carefully. By adding and stirring the liquids in afterwards, you can start a number of beakers at almost the same time. It helps to have the liquid premeasured, too.

- Why do you care about the time between starting different beakers? Because you are trying to check only the variables you are testing, and to keep everything else the same. If time becomes a "variable," it might cause some of the effects you are seeing instead of, or besides, the amount of yeast, sugar, or other thing you're testing.

- He added food coloring for fun, and so it was easier to see the differences between the different beakers. It shows up better in photos, and makes a dramatic looking presentation. If you're doing a graph or chart, you could make the colors on your chart match the colors used in your beakers. For example, if you had a beaker with blue coloring that had water, yeast, and sugar, and one with red water, yeast, sugar, and salt mixture, you could use blue and red lines on a graph to show how long it took for these different mixtures to grow.

- Before the science fair, Martin ran his experiment a couple times without the food coloring, to see if adding or leaving out the coloring would affect the results. It didn't seem to make any difference.

# MOLD

**You're A Real Fungi....** Molds and yeasts are both fungi, not plants. Living things are organized for study into large, basic groups called kingdoms. Fungi (plural of fungus) were listed in the Plant Kingdom for many years. Then scientists learned that fungi show a closer relation to animals, but are unique and separate life forms. Scientists who study fungi are called mycologists.

**Calling All Jr. Scientists...**Have you already been accused of conducting "science experiments" in your lunch box or locker? Why not learn a bit more about these molds, and get some extra credit for what comes naturally. You could try doing experiments to see what variables affect how and why molds grow. Are they harmful, or just disgusting? Mold is the reason why chemical preservatives are added to a lot of the food we buy. Other ways of preserving food include drying, freezing or refrigerating, and salting. Older students may want to study molds up close under powerful microscopes.

**We Got Culture....** Scientists call the substance on which a mold is grown a "medium," and the mold growing on it, a "culture." One way to start a culture of mold growing is to wipe your piece of bread on a dusty surface. The best way, if you want to compare the growth of mold on two pieces of bread (maybe one with preservatives, one without, or whole wheat and white), is to get the mold directly from another moldy piece of bread. That way, the fact that some molds grow at different rates from others won't be a factor.

**These Aren't Jell-O® Molds...**⚠ Molds and mushrooms are both fungi. In general, eating unidentified mold is like eating unidentified mushrooms: some are poisonous, and some are not; some are tasty, and some are not. The black, spotty, cottony and fuzzy mold commonly found on bread is one scientists call Rhizopus stolonifer, and it's somewhat toxic. Any mold you encounter won't taste very good and could easily be toxic, so discard moldy bread. Also, be careful when you open the moldy bread bag, since some molds can trigger allergies and the spores are airborne.

**Nature's Recyclers...** Fungi are an essential part of our ecosystem. They recycle millions of tons of organic waste annually, and we couldn't live without them.

**Happy Landing...** Molds reproduce by spores. Spores are like seeds; they germinate to produce a new mold colony when they land in a suitable place. Some germinate only after they are exposed to fires or freezing. Since the baking temperature would kill any spores in bread dough, you can probably assume that spores in the air (or on a counter, container or utensil) are the source of your bread's mold invasion.

**Join Me For Lunch?** Fungi have very similar metabolisms to animals, so they eat the same stuff we do. They like bread since it is rich in carbohydrates. Molds will appear sooner in natural, homemade breads because preservatives are used in commercial breads. However, additives like sorbitol don't kill fungi, they just slow down their growth so that the bread is acceptable to consumers longer.

**I'm Thirsty!** You'll probably find that bread mold grows quicker in dark, wet and warm conditions. Like all living things, molds need food, water, and proper temperature in order to grow. In fact, just like humans, molds are mostly water. The water environment of the cell allows all of the components to move and mix properly. Moisture is critical for mold's normal survival.

**I'm in the Dark!** Be careful about jumping to the conclusion that molds grow better in the light. Some may, but most molds do not need light for normal growth, because they don't make their own food like plants do. The main reason to grow molds in the dark is that they might get dried out by sun or bright light. Light would raise the temperature of the bread, making the mold warmer, and that's probably why your mold may grow better in the light than the dark.

**So you think you're pretty hot!** When it's warm, the chemical reactions causing the mold to grow happen faster than when it's cold. Therefore, the mold grows faster. Molds cannot control their temperature, so they must grow and develop at whatever temperature their environment is. For humans, the temperature at which the proteins called "enzymes" in our cells work best is 98.6°, which is our body temperature. For most molds, the optimal temperature is around 80 degrees.

**Why Study Moldy Bread?** Besides the fact that science is just plain fun, there are many

molds that affect our lives, in good ways and bad. Preparing and preserving food is just one area for research. The greatest contribution to medicine of all time came from "playing with" mold — antibiotics. The discovery of penicillin by Sir Alexander Fleming in 1928 may have saved more lives than all other medical discoveries combined.

Maybe someday …

# MUSIC

Anything as important to people's lives as bread is bound to show up in our music, and it does, around the world. There are hundreds of songs with titles about bread that have been recorded in every musical style, from Classical, Country, Jazz, and Blues, to Folk, Gospel, Reggae, Cuban, Country & Western, Rap, Punk, Ska, and of course, a number of Children's albums. A few of them are hidden in the notes on this page.

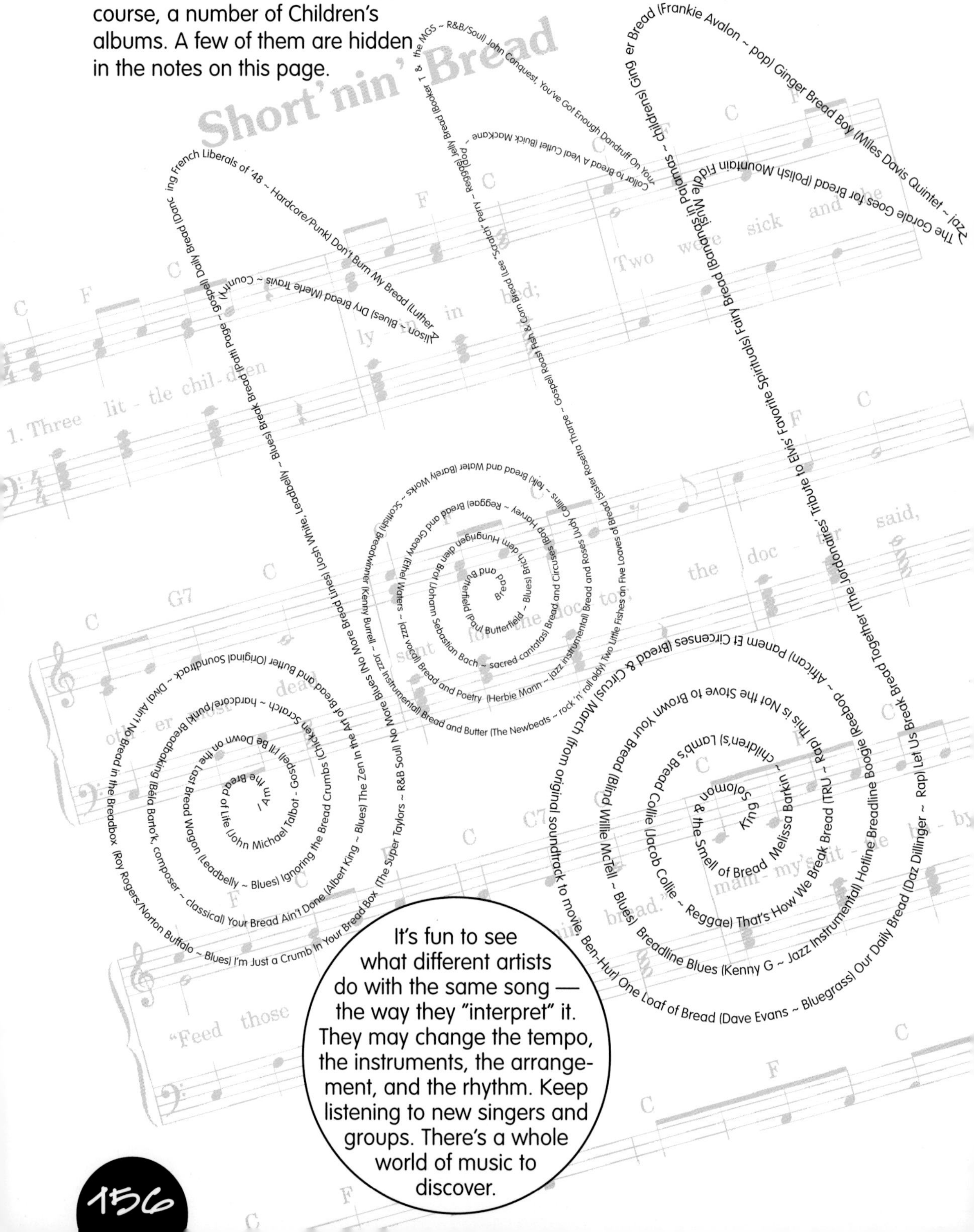

Short'nin' Bread

*Song titles arranged along the notes:*

- Ginger Bread Boy (Frankie Avalon ~ pop)
- Ginger Bread Boy (Miles Davis Quintet ~ jazz)
- The Gorale Goes for Bread (Polish Mountain Fiddle Music)
- Fairy Bread (Banana Bread) ~ children's
- Collar to Bread a Veal Cutlet (Buick MacKane ~ ...)
- ... John Conquest, You've Got Enough Dandruff On You ...
- Jelly Bread (Booker T & the MGs ~ R&B/Soul)
- Banana Bread (... ~ reggae?)
- Bread Pudding ... (Scratter Perry ~ ...)
- Don't Burn My Bread (Luther ... ~ Hardcore/Punk)
- ...ing French Liberals of '48 ~ Hardcore/Punk
- Dry Bread (Merle Travis ~ Country)
- ...lison ~ Blues) Dry Bread
- Daily Bread (Doo... ~ Gospel) Daily Bread
- Bread of Life (John Michael Talbot ~ Gospel)
- I'll Be Down on the Bread Wagon (Leadbelly ~ Blues)
- The Zen in the Art of Bread and Butter (Original Soundtrack ~ DWol Ain't No...)
- ... (Chicken Scratch ~ hardcore/punk) Breadwinning ...
- ... (Béla Bartók, composer ~ classical) Your Bread Ain't Done (Albert King ~ Blues)
- Ignoring the Bread Crumbs (The Super Taylors ~ R&B Soul)
- (Roy Rogers/Norton Buffalo ~ Blues) I'm Just a Crumb in Your Bread Box
- ... Bread in the Breadbox
- (Kenny Burrell ~ Jazz Instrumental) Bread and Butter (The Newbeats ~ rock 'n' roll)
- Apple Pie Two Little Fishes on Five Loaves of Bread ...
- No More Blues (No More Bread Lines) Lipson White, Leadbelly ~ ...
- (Paul Butterfield ~ Blues) Bread and Poetry (Herbie Mann ~ ...)
- (Johann Sebastian Bach ~ sacred cantatas) Bread and Circuses (Bob Collins)
- Brich den Hungrigen dein Brot (Johann Sebastian Bach)
- ...field Breadwinner ~ Scottish) Breadwinner
- ... Harvey ~ Reggae) Bread and Greasy Works ~ Scottish)
- Folk! Bread and Water (Barely Works ~ ...)
- ...Muddy Waters ~ Jazz vocal) ...
- (Sister Rosetta ...) Jelly Bread ...
- King Solomon
- children's) Lamb's Bread & the Smell of Bread ... Melissa Barkin
- Rap) That's How We Break Bread (TRU ~ Rap Instrumental)
- Hotline Breadline Boogie (Reebop ~ African)
- Panem Et Circenses (Bread & Circus) March (from original soundtrack to movie, Ben-Hur)
- (Blind Willie McTell ~ Blues) Breadline Blues (Kenny G ~ Jazz Instrumental)
- One Loaf of Bread (Dave Evans ~ Bluegrass)
- Our Daily Bread (Daz Dillinger ~ Rap)
- Let Us Break Bread Together (The Jordonaires' Tribute to Elvis' Favorite Spirituals)
- This is Not the Stove to Brown Your Bread (Blind Willie McTell ~ Blues)
- ... Brown Collie (Jacob Collie ~ Reggae)

*Sheet music lyrics (Shortnin' Bread):*

1. Three lit-tle chil-dren ... ly ... in bed; Two were sick and ... said, ... the doc ... "Feed those ...

---

It's fun to see what different artists do with the same song — the way they "interpret" it. They may change the tempo, the instruments, the arrangement, and the rhythm. Keep listening to new singers and groups. There's a whole world of music to discover.

156

# LANGUAGE

**Excuse me, but what did you say?** Bread has been an important food for people all over the world for thousands of years. Here are a few examples of how people say bread in different languages:

Arabic:  aish

**Danish:  brød**

Dutch:  brood

**Esperanto:  pano**

**Finnish:  leipä**

**French:  pain**

German:  Brot

Greek:  psomi'

**Hebrew:  lechem**

Hungarian:  kenyér

**Indonesian:  roti**

**Italian:  pane**

**Japanese:  pan**

Norwegian:  brød

Polish:  chleb

Portuguese:  pão

**Rumanian:  pîine**

Russian:  khlep

**Spanish:  pan**

**Swahili:  mkate**

**Swedish:  bröd**

Turkish:  ekmek

Yiddish:  broit

• When you start learning and exploring words, one thing leads to the next.  You may want to know where these languages come from, or who speaks them. People who study where our words come from and how they have developed are called "etymologists" (not to be confused with "entomologists," who study bugs).

• Isn't it interesting that there are so many different words for bread, but also that some countries use words that are almost alike?  Try listing all the words that look or sound alike in groups, like the ones close to the French word, "pain," or the German word, "brot," or the Russian "khlep." Then for each group, try to find on a map or globe the countries these languages come from.

# HOMEWORK

**What a great day we've had. Now, I want you to write an essay, in 25 words or less, explaining everything you still don't know about bread.... Just kidding.... You know I never give homework on Fridays.... Have a great weekend!**

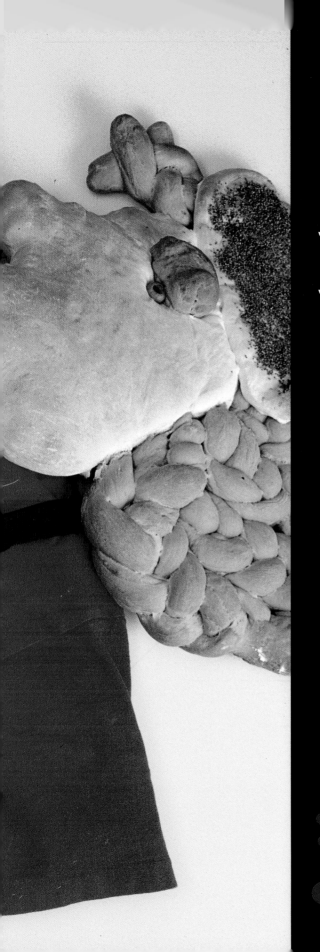

# TIPS AND TOOLS

# TIPS FROM OUR KIDS...

There are lots of little secrets in the following pages that will make your baking experience easier. Here's what our kids thought was important to share:

### Anything Yucky On Your Hands?
Be sure to wash your hands very well before you begin baking because whatever starts on your hands will probably end up in your dough. Yuck!

### Remove The Pan...
Before you begin, take the pan out of the bread machine and place it on the counter. Measure right into the pan. This will keep you from spilling inside the bread machine. Ingredients spilled into the bread machine could smoke or smell during baking.

### About Bread Flour...
The recipes in this book call for bread flour. If you don't already have bread flour at your home, you can find it in your local grocery store. Just look for the labels that say the flour is specially milled for making bread. Bread flour has a high gluten content that will give your loaves and doughs much better structure than an "all-purpose" flour.

## Baking Together...

Of course, our youngest bakers couldn't do these projects on their own, but all the test kitchen bakers learned the advantages of baking together. They helped each other read recipes and clarify directions. One fresh idea sparked a dozen more. And clean-up was a breeze when kids helped each other.

## Plan Ahead...

It's really sad when you had hoped to finish a baking project to share with your family and friends and you run out of time. Before you start a dough project, estimate how long it will take to make the dough, shape it, let it rise and then bake. If you don't have time for one recipe, choose another that takes less time. Save the more time-consuming recipe for a weekend project.

## To Make Now And Enjoy Later...

Prepare the recipe as you usually do. Shape your dough and place it in the baking pan. Then cover tightly with plastic wrap. Pre-shaped chilled or frozen

doughs must rise at room temperature until double in size, before you bake them according to the recipe instructions. (Page 26.) This is great for Cinnamon Rolls... shape, refrigerate or freeze one afternoon and serve them fresh from the oven another morning.

## Does This Make Sense?

Always use your common sense. Ask yourself: "Does this make sense to me?" (Rosey wondered once: "Would it be 1 'cup' of salt? No, that can't be right!") If something is unclear, double check with your adult helper.

### Measuring Sticky Stuff...

Before measuring sticky ingredients, lightly spray the inside of the measuring tool with non-stick cooking spray. Items like honey and molasses slide right out, without having to use a spatula to scrape them into the pan.

### About Doughs...

Different doughs have varied textures and will handle differently. Sweet dough is stickier than White so you'll need a bit more flour on your work surface. Wheat doughs are drier and less elastic and work best as loaves, braids or rolls.

### Making A Rope...

To make great long skinny ropes, hold a piece of dough between the palms of your hands and squeeze lightly along the rope. Keep an even thickness as you move your palms up and down the rope. Let gravity help you stretch the dough by allowing the rope to hang down as you make it longer. (Our kids call this "milking the cow!") Then roll the rope back and forth on the work surface for a nice smooth finish.

### Rolling A Rectangle...

Start by forming your dough ball into a rectangular shape with your hands. As you roll the dough (Page 24), it helps to pull gently on the corners to make them square. You can also gently stretch the sides to make them longer and more even.

### I Was Amazed It Was So Easy!

Every time you make a recipe in this book, all you need to do is put the ingredients into the pan in the order they are listed on the page. Start at the top and just add them in order, using only one type of yeast. That's all there is to it!

### About Eggs...

We like using egg substitutes both in our recipes and for egg wash. For health reasons, always wash your hands after handling raw eggs. Also, the delay bake cycle should not be used for recipes that contain eggs.

### Finger Push Test...

Here's another tip we learned from our chef, Tim Doebler: You can tell if your dough is ready to bake (double in size) by pushing lightly on the dough with your finger. If the dough springs back up immediately, it isn't ready. If a small impression remains, it's time to bake!

### Learn From Your Mistakes...

As any scientist will tell you, "mistakes" are opportunities to learn and improve. Some loaves that look a little "odd" taste absolutely fine. But if your loaf looks like a "hockey puck," "crater" or tastes bad, double check your measurements the next time you bake. You can also check out the original *Electric Bread*. It has great information about ingredients and troubleshooting.

163

# THE TOOL STORE

**SAVE $5 purchase kit**

## Dough Starter Kit

Everything you need to be a star with dough! Buy all of our best–selling dough tools listed below and save five dollars. $23

### Dough Roller

This multipurpose wooden roller fits in any size hand and requires less arm strength than traditional rolling pins. It's a great tool to have when throwing a Snowflake Party.   $6

### Dough Cutter

A necessity for dough lovers. It rocks and rolls against the counter top, cutting dough with the greatest of ease. And look Mom...no scratches on the counter top!   $4

### Scissors

These junior–size scissors are sharp enough to do the job, but small enough for control and saftey. Handle colors may vary.   $2

### Jr. Rolling Pin

We searched and searched for a user friendly children's wooden rolling pin that provided the weight and length neccesary to be a useful kitchen tool. Our search ended when we located this durable Jr. Rolling Pin.   $10

### Pizza Cutter

This 3-1/2-inch stainless steel blade cuts pizza crust without destroying the toppings and the EZ-Grip handle is perfect for all ages. Our kids discovered it was the best tool to use when cutting dough strips in May Baskets, Pretzels and Fall Harvest Breadsticks.   $6

## Baking Rings

We spied an important tool for any successful Super Sleuth Party. This set of four baking rings is used to shape the eye of the Magnifying Glasses on Page 118. When you're not sleuthing, use them as biscuit cutters, egg rings, or even to make English muffins.    $5

## Woolie Mitts

These 100% wool oven mitts are made in the USA and are a sensational hit with the kids in the *Electric Bread* Test Kitchen. They are the perfect size for young hands wanting to help without getting burned. The  colors  are  fabulous too!    $30

## TO ORDER CALL
## 1-800-541-2733

## Flour Leveler

This may be the best $1.50 you ever spend to accurately measure ingredients. Simply wipe the straight edge of the Flour Leveler across the top of your dry ingredients to ensure a true measurement.    $1.50

## Wooden Toaster Tongs

Is toasted bread a favorite of yours? Keep it safe when removing slices from your toaster with our wooden Toaster Tongs. They're so simple we wonder why no one thought of it sooner!    $4

## The Electric Bread Apron

Look like a pro in the kitchen while keeping your clothes clean with this machine washable 3–pocket apron.The *Electric Bread* Apron looks fabulous on just about anyone, including our Kitchen Witch on Page 158!    $16

## Personal Size Pizza Pans

Bring that deep dish pizza taste into your kitchen with this set of four personal size pizza pans. Chicago Metallic's heavyweight pans are used by professionals for their durability and superb quality. Includes manufacturer's recipe book.   $20

## Mini Bread Pans

Chicago Metallic's Mini Bread Pans produce fabulous loaves. These pans are a great way to give your daily bread a different look—try a mini loaf for each family member at dinner instead of dinner rolls. $12/set of 4 and $18/set of 6.

## Dough Sheet

Ever have a hard time rolling your cinnamon rolls out into a 12–inch by 18–inch rectangle? Well those days are gone. Say hello to the *Electric Bread* Dough Sheet! This woven cloth has ruler borders and three circle sizes clearly marked to make rolling dough a snap. And it gives you a head start with cleanup. A must for the precise baker.   $25

## TO ORDER CALL
# 1-800-541-2733

Our *Electric Bread* Party Kits are here! Each kit is designed to help you host a party for you and five friends with invites, recipe cards, activities and party favors. Discover how easy it can be to throw an *Electric Bread* Party! $75/Kit

### Circus Party...
This kit will help you prepare a Circus Party like the one on Page 120. Complete with balloons to use for invitations, recipe cards, popcorn bags, a face painting kit, and six food Color Paste sets (Page 169) for party favors.

### Super Sleuth Party...
Invite your "sleuthing" friends over for a treasure hunt and make the beautiful Magnifying Glasses on Page 118. This kit includes coded invitations, treasure hunt ideas, recipe cards, and Jolly Ranchers®. Six Sprinkle Canisters and Baking Rings for party favors will make your sleuthing party the best mystery night ever.

### Pizza Party...
Ready for a Pizza Party like ours on Page 128? You will be with this kit. It contains pizza shaped invitations, recipe cards, a dough roller, and six EZ Grip Pizza Cutters for party favors.

### Snowflake Party...
When the weather gets chilly, come inside for a break and throw a Snowflake Party like Emily did on Page 116. This kit contains invitations, recipe cards, and a small strainer for powdered sugar. Your guests will get a Dough Roller and a pair of Scissors to make dough snowflakes at their own home.

### Space Party...
Explore the final frontier with your closest friends and design the inhabitants along the way. This kit contains everything for the great Space Party on Page 124. Invitations, recipe cards, glow-in-the-dark star stickers, a Dough Roller and two sets of Color Pastes will help you make Space Alien Heads come alive in your kitchen. Each guest will go home with their very own set of headboppers and scissors in case they want to blast off under their own power.

## Wooden Bread Slicer

Use this hardwood slicer to produce uniform 1/2-inch slices every time. Its large size accommodates almost any loaf, making it exactly what you need when slicing bread fresh from your machine.　$13

## Farberware® Slice & Store

This product combines air tight bread storage with a convenient slicing tray that can also be used for serving. Microwave, freezer, and dishwasher safe.　$15

## The Perfect Beaker

Uniquely shaped, this easy–to–read liquid measuring beaker is perhaps the most important kitchen tool. The two cup capacity beaker has markings from teaspoons to cups, including metric. You'll know the first time you use it why it's known around town as the "Perfect Beaker."　$6

## Assorted Sprinkles

Kids love these sprinkles on all their creations: Magnifying Glasses, Valentine's Day Heart, Last Year's Bread, Bread As Art. Each jar is themed with an assortment of six different sprinkles. Choose from Holiday, Crystals, Hearts & Flowers, or Fun Shapes. Better yet—order them all!　$5 each

## TO ORDER CALL
# 1-800-541-2733

## Color Pastes

The colored doughs used throughout this book are made from Wilton food color paste sets. Simply add a dab to the water when starting your machine. The Color Pastes are available in a Pastel Color Set containing pink, peach, light green, and pale blue or a Primary Color Set of yellow, red, blue, and brown.

$5 per set, Pastel or Primary.

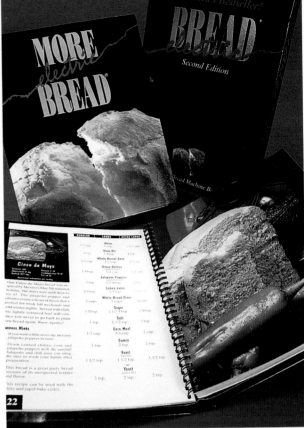

*Electric Bread®* **and** *More Electric Bread®*
Experience more of our test kitchen magic with *Electric Bread* and *More Electric Bread.* Both feature incredible gourmet bread recipes with full-color photography. *Electric Bread* is ideal for the new bread machine owner, while *More Electric Bread* is perfect for the advanced baker who wants to experiment with doughs like bagels, baguettes, and strudel. The perfect gift for your adult helper! $29.95 each.

## Fancy Bread Tubes

Wouldn't you love this bread as a snack the next time your friends are over? Peanut butter and jelly never looked so fancy. You simply let the dough rise in the greased tube, bake, slice, and enjoy. $20/set of 3

## Bear Bun Warmer

A unique way of keeping bread warm at the table, this little bear is microwaved and then placed in a basket to keep rolls and sliced bread warm during meals. $5

# TEST KITCHEN TEAM

Executive Chef: **Tim Doebler,** C.W.C., C.C.E.
Education Specialist: **Ann McKay Bryson**

Test Kitchen Manager: **Kathy Ebel**
Team Adviser: **Mary Ann Swalling**

These young bakers spent hundreds of hours together in our test kitchen creating, testing and tasting the recipes and bread activities featured in this book:

**Courtney Bernard**
**Kati Bryson**
**Molly Bryson**
**Rosey Bryson**
**Kelsey Cloud**
**Jamie Crimp**
**Matthew Crimp**

**Amy Glen**
**Sarah Glen**
**Erin Eggleston**
**Galen Eggleston**
**Sam Friedman**
**Jayme Jaime**
**Marisa Jaso**

**Cale Jorgensen**
**Quinsey Jorgensen**
**Monica Kompkoff**
**Nyaling Marenah**
**Tiana Marenah**
**Cameron McKay**
**Martin McKay**

**Emily McLaughlir**
**Andrew Merrell**
**Joanna Onorat**
**Michael Onorat**
**Corey Russell**
**Justin Siemens**
**Kyle Siemens**
**Aly Shroy**

## ICE Cold Testers

This group volunteered to double check the recipes and activities before our book went to print:

Grethe Denkewalter
Andy Christopherson
Ashley Christopherson
James Dooley
Meghan Dooley

Jaime Faulkner
Alex Kubitz
Max Kubitz
Alli Machacek

Wilson Middleton
Jake Schneider
Ben Schneider
Chase Swalling

Christian Swalling
Rosie Thompson
Carrie Williamson
Patrick Wolgemuth
Rilee Sue Yandt

*In recognition of the unselfish contributions of all the kids who worked with us in our test kitchen, Innovative Cooking Enterprises is donating a portion of the proceeds from the sale of each copy of* **Electric Bread for Kids** *to charities that help children.*

*We were blessed with the help of many old and new friends
as we developed **Electric Bread for Kids**,
and wish to acknowledge their astounding talents and generosity.*

*In particular, the enthusiasm and creativity of all the kids
who baked in our test kitchen was an inspiration.
Behind these young stars were families
whose tremendous efforts made it possible for the kids
to have great fun, and for us to produce this book.*

*To our own families and loved ones…
for the words of encouragement you gave,
for the other words you spared us,
for the endless little favors and big sacrifices,
for your confidence and your hugs, we can't thank you enough.
But we'll try.*

*Making this book brought our families together.
We hope using it will do the same for yours.*

## Technical Assistance

George Bryson
Color Art Printing
Mary Jo Exley
Shirley Laird
Lanrie Leung
Patti McBride
Sasha Sagan
Vladimir Pavlenko
Fran Brink
Frank Flavin
Greg Forte, C.E.C., C.C.E.
Debbie Phelps-Jaso
Debra Ann Schneider

## Project Support

Habitat
Donna Alderman
Butterfields
Design Craft
Jim Dobbelaire
Frankel & Summers
Kim Holm
Jill Kolberg
Metro Books & Music
Metro Home Furnishings
Romney Dodd-Ortland
Stephen Ortland
Chris Swalling

## Special Projects
Lara Parrish

**Special Thanks To:**
MOA Summer Playground Class of Susan Malecha and Todd Wimer

# INDEX